The outdoor market in Eisiskes, 1914, prior to World War I. Photographer: Yitzhak Uri Katz. Public domain, source: Wikimedia Commons.

Mill on the Virshoky River, 1930. Public domain, source: Wikimedia Commons.

Ejszyszki, its History and Destruction (Eišiškes, Lithuania)

Translation of
Eishishok, koroteha ve-hurbana

Original Book Edited by: Sh. Barkeli

Originally published in Jerusalem 1960

JewishGen
מרכז עולמי לגנאלוגיה יהודית
The Global Home for Jewish Genealogy

A Publication of JewishGen
Edmond J. Safra Plaza, 36 Battery Place, New York, NY 10280
646.494.2972 | info@JewishGen.org | www.jewishgen.org

MUSEUM OF
JEWISH HERITAGE
A LIVING MEMORIAL
TO THE HOLOCAUST

Ejszyszki, its History and Destruction
Translation of *Eishishok, koroteha ve-hurbana*

Copyright © 2024 by JewishGen. All rights reserved.
First Printing: May 2024, Iyar, 5784
Editor of Original Yizkor Book: Sh. Barkeli
Project Coordinator: Judy Bston
Cover Design: Nina Schwartz, Impulse Graphics
Layout: Jonathan Wind
Name Indexing: Jonathan Wind

JewishGen Press is not responsible for inaccuracies or omissions in the original work and makes no representations regarding the accuracy of this translation. Digital images of the original book's contents can be seen online at the New York Public Library website or the Yiddish Book Center website.

Library of Congress Control Number (LCCN): 2022952300

ISBN: 978-1-954176-68-3 (hard cover: 186 pages, alk. paper)

About Jewishgen.org

Jewishgen, is a Genealogical Research Division of the Museum of Jewish Heritage - A Living Memorial to the Holocaust, serves as the global home for Jewish genealogy.

Featuring unparalleled access to 30+ million records, it offers unique search tools, along with opportunities for researchers to connect with others who share similar interests. Award winning resources such as the Family Finder, Discussion Groups, and ViewMate, are relied upon by thousands each day.

In addition, Jewishgen's extensive informational, educational and historical offerings, such as the Jewish Communities Database, Yizkor Book translations, InfoFiles, Family Tree of the Jewish People, and KehilaLinks, provide critical insights, first-hand accounts, and context about Jewish communal and familial life throughout the world.

Offered as a free resource, Jewishgen.org has facilitated thousands of family connections and success stories, and is currently engaged in an intensive expansion effort that will bring many more records, tools, and resources to its collections.

Please visit https://www.jewishgen.org/ to learn more.

Vice President for JewishGen: Avraham Groll

About the JewishGen Yizkor Book Project

Yizkor Books (Memorial Books) were traditionally written to memorialize the names of departed family and martyrs during holiday services in the synagogue (a practice that still exists in many synagogues today).

Over the centuries, as a result of countless persecutions and horrific atrocities committed against the Jews, Yizkor Books (Sefer Zikaron in Hebrew) were expanded to include more historical information, such as biographical sketches of famous personalities and descriptions of daily town life.

Following the Holocaust, the idea of remembrance and learning took on an urgent and crucial importance. Survivors of the Holocaust sought out other surviving residents of their former towns to memorialize and document the names and way of life of those who were ruthlessly murdered by the Nazis. These remembrances were documented in Yizkor Books, hundreds of which were published in the first decades after the Holocaust.

Most of these books were published privately, or through Landsmanshaftn (social organizations comprised of members originating from the same European town or region) that still existed, and were often distributed free of charge. The languages used to document these crucial histories and links to our past were mostly Yiddish and Hebrew. JewishGen has undertaken the sacred responsibility of translating these books into English so that the culture and way of life of these communities will be preserved and transmitted to future generations.

In 1986, a group of farsighted JewishGenners started a project to pool their efforts together in groups based upon their ancestors' towns and donate funds to translate the Yizkor books of their ancestral towns into English. As the translated material became available, it was made accessible for free at https://www.JewishGen.org/Yizkor .

Hardcover copies can be purchased by visiting https://www.jewishgen.org/Yizkor/ybip.html (see below).

It is our hope that the translation of these books into English (and other languages) will assist the countless Jewish family researchers who are so desperately seeking to forge a connection with their heritage.

Director of JewishGen Yizkor Book Project: Lance Ackerfeld

About JewishGen Press

JewishGen Press (formerly the Yizkor Books-in-Print Project) is the publishing division of JewishGen.org, and provides a venue for the publication of non-fiction books pertaining to Jewish genealogy, history, culture, and heritage.

In addition to the Yizkor Book category, publications in the Other Non-Fiction category include Shoah memoirs and research, genealogical research, collections of genealogical and historical materials, biographies, diaries and letters, studies of Jewish experience and cultural life in the past, academic theses, and other books of interest to the Jewish community.

Please visit https://www.jewishgen.org/Yizkor/ybip.html to learn more.

Director of JewishGen Press: Joel Alpert
Managing Editor - Jessica Feinstein
Publications Manager - Susan Rosin

Notes to the Reader

The images in the original book were reproduced from photographs from the time of the first edition. These reproductions were already of poor quality, being pre-war and at least 30 or more years old. As a result, the images in the book are the best achievable.

A reader can view the original scans of the book on the websites listed below.

The original book can be seen online at the Yiddish Book Center website:

https://www.yiddishbookcenter.org/collections/yizkor-books/yzk-nybc314188/alufi-perets-barkali-eshishok-koroteha-ve-hurbanah-pirke-zikronot-ve-aduyot

OR

at the New York Public Library Digital Collections website:

https://digitalcollections.nypl.org/items/963cb070-7423-0133-02f6-00505686d14e

To obtain a list of Shoah victims from **Ejszyszki (Eišiškes, Lithuania)**, the reader should access the Yad Vashem web site listed below; one can also search for specific family names using family name option. These lists are continually updated by Yad Vashem, so it is worthwhile to periodically search these.

There is more valuable information (including the Pages of Testimony, etc.) available on this website:
https://yvng.yadvashem.org/

Additional resources for Ejszyszki and the surrounding areas are:

https://kehilalinks.jewishgen.org/Lida-District/eisiskes.htm

The Eisiskes Kehilalink page at JewishGen.org contains a list of Eisiskes Pages of Testimony

The LitvakSIG Lida District Research Group (LitvakSIG.org), which has translated nearly 150,000 Jewish records from Eisiskes and nearby towns.

A list of all books available from JewishGen Press along with prices is available at:
https://www.jewishgen.org/Yizkor/ybip.html

Cover Photo Credits

Cover Design by: Nina Schwartz, Impulse Graphics

Front cover:

Friends pose on the steps of Alte Katz's pharmacy, c.1933-38. Photographer: Ben-Zion Szrejder. Source: United States Holocaust Memorial Museum, courtesy of The Shtetl Foundation. Right to left: Esther (Etele) Katz, her sister Shoshana, and their friend Fania Botwiniki. Seated on steps, right to left: Avigdor Katz, Yitzhak Sonenson, Gittele Sonenson, and two friends. To the right of the steps is the entrance to the bakery below street level. To the left, a display of photos from the Katz photography studio.

Noyach Schevitzky, c.1900. Courtesy of Roz Sherman Voellinger.

The marketplace, Eišiškės, 1914-17. Peasants and townspeople shop at the central market square during the German occupation of World War I. Public domain, source: Wikimedia Commons.

Back Cover:

From top right:

Electrical power plant building, 1931. Photographer: Rephael Lejbowicz. Public domain, source: Wikimedia Commons. Standing in front, left to right: Shlomo Kiuchefski, Dora Zlotnik Berkowicz, Zeev Kaganowicz, and his wife, Masha (née Kiuchefski). The power plant was built and owned by the Kiuchefski family and Moshe Kaganowicz.

Zlatta and Yossel Bass at the gravestone of Zlatta's father, Eli Dovid Schevitzky, 1921. Courtesy of Roz Sherman Voellinger. The writing on the gravestone says: Our dear father, honest and honorable; and gives the death date as 26 Av 5680 (10 August 1920).

Bluma Jurdyczanski and her niece Leah'le Dugaczinski stroll down Vilna Street, c.1938. Source: United States Holocaust Memorial Museum, courtesy of The Shtetl Foundation.

Leon (Nacham Leib) Shlansky poses in skis on a snowy street, c.1938. Source: United States Holocaust Memorial Museum, courtesy of The Shtetl Foundation.

Geopolitical Information

Map of Lithuania showing the location of **Eišiškes**

Ejszyszki Geopolitical Information

Eišiškes, Lithuania is located at 54°10' N 25°00' E and 38 miles SSW of Vilnius.

	Town	District	Province	Country
Before WWI (c. 1900):	Eishishki	Lida	Vilna	Russian Empire
Between the wars (c. 1930):	Ejszyszki	Lida	Nowogródek	Poland
After WWII (c. 1950):	Eišiškės			Soviet Union
Today (c. 2000):	Eišiškės			Lithuania

Alternate Names for the Town:

Eišiškės [Lith], Eshishuk [Yid], Ejszyszki [Pol], Eishishki [Rus], Eišišķes [Latv], Aisheshuk, Aishishak, Aishishuk, Eishishuk, Eishyshok, Eyshishkes, Eyshishok, Aišiškės

Nearby Jewish Communities:

Radun, Belarus 8 miles S
Voranava, Belarus 14 miles E
Valkininkai 14 miles NNW
Byenyakoni, Belarus 16 miles ENE
Degsnės 16 miles NNW
Varėna 18 miles W
Šalčininkai 18 miles ENE
Lieponys 22 miles NNW

Lida, Belarus 23 miles SSE
Jašiunai 24 miles NE
Dieveniškės 25 miles E
Panošiškes 26 miles NNW
Onuškis 27 miles NW
Vasilishki, Belarus 27 miles SSW
Lipnishki, Belarus 28 miles ESE
Daugai 30 miles WNW

Table of Contents

The Destruction of Eishishok

Miscellaneous

Name Index

Ejszyszki, its History and Destruction (Eišiškes, Lithuania)

54°10' / 25°00'

Translation of
Eishishok, koroteha ve-hurbana

Editor: Sh. Barkeli

Published in Jerusalem 1960

Acknowledgments:

Our sincere appreciation to Kenneth Juris who has kindly donated this translation for online presentation on the JewishGen web site.

Translated in 1980 from the Hebrew by Shoshanna Gavish.

Copy editing and proofreading by Judy Baston

Text scanning by Seth Morgulas.

This is a translation of: *Eishishok, koroteha ve-hurbana* (Ejszyszki, its history and destruction), Editor: Sh. Barkeli, Committee of the Survivors of Ejszyszki in Israel, Published: Jerusalem 1960 (H,Y 136 pages).

Note: The original book can be seen online at the NY Public Library site: Eisiskes

אישישוק

קורותיה וחורבנה

פרקי זכרונות ועדויות (בצרוף תמונות)

ליקט וסידר

פרץ אלופי

ערך

ד"ר שאול ברקלי

יוצא לאור על־ידי

הועד לניצולי אישישוק במדינת ישראל

ירושלים, תשי"ד

<u>YIZKOR</u>

This book contains the history of the small Jewish town
Called Eishishok (Yiddish) Ejszyszki (Polish) Eisiskes (Russian)
Located approximately 35 miles south-southwest of Vilna,
Lithuania
and destroyed by the Nazis and their collaborators
During World War II

**Translated in 1980 from the Hebrew by Shoshanna
Gavish**

Translation commissioned by Kenneth Juris
Who donated the translation to JewishGen

Copy editing and proofreading by Judy Baston

Photograph captions translated by Sara Mages

"Eishishok"
Its history and its destruction
Documentaries, memoirs and illustrations
Compiled and edited by Peretz Alufi and Dr. Shaul Barkali
Published through the Committee of Survivors of Eishishok
in Israel, Jerusalem, Israel 1950

Memorial Prayer

May the people of Israel and their G-d remember the 4,000 souls of the sons and daughters of the community of Eishishok as well as the souls of those that were brought from neighboring communities and which includes infants and children, men and women who were all holy and pure and among them great scholars of the Torah and people of good deeds, people who followed the path of G-d, honestly and righteously, that were murdered by the hands of the Nazis and their Lithuanian and Polish assistants on the fourth and fifth day of the Hebrew month of Tishre in the year 5702. Their hearts cry towards the heavens and demand that their lives which were cut short before their time be remembered, "Earth, don't cover their blood, and let their cries forever be heard and not forgotten May their souls be bound in the land of the everlasting life. Rest in Peace."

[Page V]

Introduction

When the terrible news of the tragic deaths of the Jews of the city of Eishishok by the hands of the impure Nazis was verified by the refugees who survived the destruction and arrived in Israel, a Committee was formed in Jerusalem under the initiative of Naphtali Berkowitz, Moshe Kaganowicz and Uri Rozovsky to commemorate the pain and suffering felt by the destruction of their community.

A convention was held on the 23rd of Chesvan 5706, shortly after the first refugees of Eishishok arrived in Israel. Among those attending were those from Eishishok but already residing in Israel and including Rabbi Meir Stalitz, Dov Dechasalvitz, the chief of Zichron Moshe in Jerusalem, the great scholar Rabbi Chaim Paltiel and others. After a memorial prayer and eulogy, a committee was formed whose headquarters would be in Jerusalem, which was the residence of most of the survivors. The main function of the committee was to support and aid the survivors of the city who would immigrate to Israel after their many hardships that had befallen them.

Uri Rozovsky, Naphtali Berkowitz, Zessel Chensky, Yosef Goldstein, Rivka Shenzer, Chaim Levyatan, Avram Schmuel Gross, Nachum Radunsky (Petach Tikvah) and Chaya Reznik (Tel Aviv) were elected to work on the committee. From this group, an executive committee was formed A. Rozovsky-Chairman , Z. Chensky-Secretary, N. Berkowitz-Treasurer, Y. Goldstein-Associate. Sholom Sonenson was added to the committee when he arrived in Israel.

The committee collected monthly dues, the sum of which was distributed among the refugees of Eishishok who arrived in Israel. It was at this time the committee corresponded with the "Natives of Eishishok in Boston" and with the "Committee to aid Citizens of Eishishok in New York" from whom they received large amounts of money and distributed to the needy refugees.

During the second convention which was held on the fourth of Tishre, 5707 in Jerusalem, it was decided to follow the suggestion of Dr. Saul Barkali , a native of our city, to publish a compilation to commemorate the community of Eishishok. A committee was formed to take care of all the matters which would be involved in the publishing to this compilation. The members of the committee were: Dr. Saul Barkali (Kaleko) , S. Sonenson,and Perez Alufi (Kaleko). Dr. Barkali and P. Alufi volunteered to gather all the material and do the compilation.

A letter was sent to all the natives of Eishishok in Israel and the Diaspora which requested their participation in the compilation by writing memoirs, testimonials, notes, etc. about their city from its past to its last day. Also, they were requested to aid the committee by sending donations to pay for the publishing of the compilation. The decision to publish the compilation was accepted with goodwill and sympathy by all the natives of Eishishok in the Diaspora and Israel and as a result much material was accumulated.

It is appropriate to make special mention of the "Natives of Eishishok in Boston" and the "Committee to aid Citizens of Eishishok in New York" for their generous contributions for making publishing of this compilation possible and for raising funds for a memorial tablet to commemorate our dearly beloved holy ones for us and for the forthcoming generations.

Committee For The Aiding of Survivors of Eishishok
Uri Rozovsky, Chairman
Zessel Chensky, Secretary
Naphtali Berkowitz. Treasurer
Yosef Goldstein, Member of Committee

[Page VII]

Foreword

Recognizing the great responsibility we took upon ourselves to edit this compilation in the memory of the Eishishok community, so dear to our hearts. Our desire was to set up a memorial and monument in Israel's community even though the community of Eishishok was not considered one of the larger communities according to the number of Jews living there. However, it was famous in Lithuania and Russia as one of the great 11 cities of learning in the previous country.

We split the material available to us into two main parts: A. Eishishok in the past and B. Eishishok in its last years up to the day of its complete destruction on the 4th and 5th days of Tishre, 5702. All the records, books and documents of the various organizations that were active in the city, and which could provide a clear and complete picture of the Jews in Eishishok in the past were destroyed along with its residents. We therefore gathered information for the compilation from old newspaper articles and books which date back as far as 80-100 years ago. We also gathered information from Polish and German encyclopedias. We also received important information from the few elder survivors of the city who are still alive in Israel.

From these sources we succeeded to obtain a picture of the cultural, economic and religious life of our community in the previous generations. As for the second part, the complete information was obtained from the survivors of the city who arrived in Israel and who are living witness to the destruction of our city and and who saw the suffering of our brothers and sisters under the bloody rule of the Nazis and their Lithuanian helpers up to the very last tragic days. The information obtained was recorded as told without adding any literary style. The words will speak for themselves. In order to enable the people who do not understand Hebrew to read the material a translation into Yiddish is also provided.

We regret very much not including all the material provided to us, but the space in the compilation was limited. To all those who provided information we thank you your help and support in this work.

May the memory of Reb Meir Stalitz and Reb Mordechai Kaleko be blessed, two of the natives of Eishishok who lived in Israel and died before this compilation was completed.

Last, but not least, we are greatly thankful to the members of the Committee of the Survivors of Eishishok in Jerusalem and to Mr. Naphtali Berkowitz, one of the community members who aided us unselfishly and made this publication possible.

The Publishers
1960

The Great Synagogue in Eishishok (1911)

[Page 3]

Eishishok in the Past

Beginnings

The beginnings of Eishishok are obscure as are those of many other small and medium sized towns of the wide plain between the rivers Niemen, Viliya and their streams. This area was largely overgrown with thick forests and green meadows running over thousands of square kilometers.

The Russian general encyclopedia (Brokhoize-Efron) informs us that Eishishok was founded by the Lithuanian military commander Aishis in 1070 and named Aishiskas after him. According to this version, Eishishok was founded about 300 years before Vilna, which was founded by Gedimin, the great Lithuanian prince (1341-1316). Apparently, Eishishok also preceded Lida, also founded by Gedimin and lately become capital of the district.

It is difficult to assess the economic and strategic importance of the town in that period. Eishishok is surrounded by no natural fortifications. There are no important mountains or rivers powerful enough to carry boats or rafts. It's importance came later when it was situated on the main transportation route connecting the fortified cities of the Lithuanian princedom: Vilna-Lida-Novogrodek. In any event, we do know that Eishishok was capital of the district for hundreds of years and the great Lithuanian prince Vitold (14th century) erected a Catholic church in the adjacent town Yourzdiki. (In Eishishok there was no Christian Church).

Over the years, Eishishok passed from one political power to another according to the political situation in the area. Thus, in 1569 Eishishok was an estate of the Polish king while 200 years later in 1771, its owner was Prince Joseph Solohor, of White-Russian origin.

Following the division of the Polish state (at the end of the 18th century), all of the Vilna region including Eishishok was transferred to the Russians. Eishishok was subsequently part of the Lida district in the Vina region. When Poland was re-established in 1918 following the First World War, Eishishok was annexed to Poland and became part of the Novogrodek region.

[Page 4]

The Beginning of the Jewish Community In Eishishok

The Polish general encyclopedia of 1883 informs us that Karaites lived in Eishishok back in 1145, that is, many years before the big Karaite community in Troki was founded in the 14th century. Thus, though we have no other evidence that a Jewish community existed in Eishishok at that time, we may nevertheless assume that the Jewish community there dates far back and is probably among the first to exist in Lithuania.

The presence of the Jews in Lithuania back in the 9th and 10th centuries is confirmed in several documents. The Prague Bishop Adalbert who was sent in 997 to preach the new covenant to idol worshipers in Lithuania, wrote the "many Christian prisoners were sold to Jews because of avarice and we have no means to ransom them".

It is also known that both Prince Gedimin (1321) and his grandson Vitold (1341) gave rights to the Jews in Lithuania. Vitold published a special Jewish law which had 37 sections and was meant to define the relations between the Jewish inhabitants of Brisk, Troki, Horodna, Lotzk, Meretsh and other places. There is no doubt that the Jewish community of Eishishok was among them.

The elders of Eishishok claim that they themselves saw in the old cemetery, tombstones dating back 600 years ago. Exact information concerning the numbers of Jews in Eishishok, their profession and public institutions, we find only from later centuries, particularly the 19th century when Eishishok became a renowned center for the study of Torah and learned Rabbis. According to one source, there were approximately 660 Jews in Eishishok in 1847 but fifty years later in 1897, during the general population count in Russia, the number grew to 2376 and constituted 70 percent of the population of the area.

The growth cannot be attributed to natural increase only. The Jewish population of Eishishok in 1897, included many Yeshiva boys. The Jewish community also absorbed the country Jews who were forbidden to live in the villages by order of the 1882 "May Laws".

More details of Jewish migrations in the Eishishok district were listed in the old register of the burial company which was burnt in the " great fire" of 1895.

It is interesting to note that the increase in the Eishishok Jewish population came to a nearly total standstill at the beginning of the 20th century. Many left to make a living in the countries of the sea, in the regional city Vilna and in other Lithuanian and Polish cities. According to the Polish count of 1921 (which, though not particularly accurate, is the only relatively reliable source for numbers), there were only 1591 Jews in the town, a decrease to 65% of the general population.

The appearance of Eishishok of 70-80 years ago is described by Mr. Yaapaz, an Eishishok Yeshiva student, in the paper HaShahar (Dawn) of the year 5639 and also by the Hatzofe editor Horshai Freedman in his book "My Memoirs " .

The following years brought great changes to the appearance of the town. After the great fire of 1895 which nearly completely destroyed Eishishok, the town was rebuilt, many brick houses were erected, the streets became straight and tiled and pavements were later laid. The main road connecting Warsaw with Vilna passed through the town and thus the formerly remote town (the nearest station in Bastuny being 24 km away), was now situated on an important crossroad and full of traffic . The town merchants, no longer satisfied with the merchandise available in Vilna or Lida, now reached Bialystok and Warsaw, the biggest industrial and commercial centers in the country.

The Eishishok Surroundings

Situated in the great plain of Lithuania, Eishishok was not surrounded by high mountains or wide rivers. Only the two streams of the " Hakantil" and " Hoyrshoki" wound round it and disappeared in a horizon edged by dark forest shadows. The two closest forests, " Seklutzki" and " the Big Forest" were more than a kilometer away. In our childish eyes, the big far miraculous world began behind the " Councillary" Building (the town's municipality) located on the crossroads of the Vilna road and the road leading to the " Yourzdiki" village and the Catholic church. But, there were three places which attracted us in their atmosphere of myth and mystery.

[Page 7]

The Old Cemetery

Amid wide fields far from the town, behind " the Big Forest",' rose a long wide stretch of land, approximately 30 meters wide and 100 meters long, overgrown with low wild bushes, Most of the tombstones were deeply sunken in the land and those few Hebrew lettered stones were barely distinguishable. These are the remnants of " the old cemetery" which had not been used by the Jews for 200 years. In our days, one could reach the cemetery by using the Vilna road, through the meadows behind the bridge on the Virshoky River, along the Yourzdiki village and thence via the road to Voronova village to the Seklotzky forest and thence down through the field paths.

But this way was dangerous for us children since there was the possibility of encountering gentiles with vicious dogs. We never ventured so far without adult accompaniment.

The elders claim that in early years a shorter and safer way was used, from the alley of the new cemetery, through the fields to the " Hakantil" river, over the bridge and straight to the old cemetery. But in our time this way was impassable. Both sides of the Hakantil were overgrown with trees and bushes hiding it from sight and a large deep swamp made passage impossible. The

Hakantil was visible only from near the bath house where the women liked to wash their linen and the children to play on its smooth stones.

There was no alternative to using the long dangerous road adjacent to the gentile village. One hot summer Sabbath, a group of us decided to take the risk and attempt to see the old cemetery with our own eyes. Our hearts were thumping with fear when we passed the dangerous stretch by the Seklotzky forest. As on every Sabbath, the forest was the gathering place of young men and women and the sounds of their merriment resounded. We bore right, passed through the tall corn and a few moments later were facing the cemetery which rose about two meters above the fields and was surrounded by a deep ditch, from that place one could see the whole town with perfect visibility. The two yeshivas were especially prominent and heading them stood the big synagogue with its three roofs, one above the other like three hats on the head.

The land was hard and barren - there were no signs of mounds or graves. A few stones were scattered interwoven with bushes and thorns. The "expert" among us pointed to the place where horses, brought to plow the cemetery land, twice broke their legs…There is a legend about the cemetery and the story is the following: When the old cemetery became too small to absorb all the village dead, a new land was acquired, closer to the village. This was the new cemetery, which lay behind the synagogue court. The old cemetery remained lonely and deserted among the harvest fields of the gentiles. These latter eventually began annexing parts of the cemetery and ploughing there. All appeals to the farmers of the district authorities to avoid desecrating the memories of the righteous buried there for centuries, were in vain. The farmers continued their ploughing and the cemetery became smaller, while the Jews looked on in despair.

Then the miracle happened. One day, a farmer who was a renowned Jew hater, again began ploughing the cemetery ground. But as his horse stepped into the cemetery, it fell and broke two legs though there were no holes or howes in the particular spot.

When the farmer returned with another horse-the same happened. This recurred several times until the farmer realized the " accidents" were not accidental at all. Fear of the G-d of Israel fell upon them and they ceased ploughing there. Thus the old cemetery was saved. It remained in loneliness and wilderness for 200 years surrounded by gentile fields, overlooking the village for afar, till the days of terror and destruction-the 4th and 5th of Tishre, 3702 (1942). Then again, it was filled with cries of thousands of Jews, men, women and children, led to slaughter by beasts in human form, again the parched earth soaked the blood of pious Jews. Four thousand holy bodies of tortured and murdered Jews found their final rest alongside the bones of their ancestors.

[Page 9]

The Maiak (Fortress)

One of the places we children loved most was the " Maiak". On Saturdays and holidays, we loved playing hide and seek or thieves and policemen in its deep channels - overgrown with bushes and trees, among them raspberry and bloodberry bushes. One of our favorite sports was running down its steep slopes to the opposite side where the wheat fields lay. Often this sport ended with torn trousers or a bloody nose but the dizzying run, which required lots of courage, not all of the boys were able to muster, made us forget the punishment awaiting us for our torn clothing.

It was said that the " Maiak" was erected by Napoleon during his invasion of Russia and that the Poles greatly fortified it during their great uprising against the Russians over 100 years ago. The mountain was not a natural one - it was man-made as was evident from its ring-like shape enclosing a rather large plain and surrounded by deep channels approximately 50 meters deep. There was only one entrance, from North, via a bridge crossing the channel. This bridge used to be lifted every evening by iron chains and then the Maiak was inaccessible.

In our time there was no trace of the bridge. The channels were overgrown with trees and bushes. In the court there remained a few buildings formerly belonging to the owner of Maiak-the landowner, Seklotzky. These houses were empty and half ruined and we played there often, increasing the ruin. Of the towers, only one ruin remained. On the north-west side, hidden among trees and bushes, arose on stone-heap, surrounded by mounds of earth and stones, which testified to the former massivity of the tower. The " Maiak" was a favorite gathering place of the Eishishok youth. There they held meetings of the " Hashomer Hatzair", " Hachalutz", the club in memory of Brener, " Herut ve Techiya" and others. Also, its scenic corners were a common place for picture taking and during the Sabbath and holidays, the air resounded with the sounds of youth rejoicing.

However, one year Maiak was chosen as the seat of the former Polish general, Dr. Riligion, Jewish children were forbidden access, and the attractive "Maiak", so full of memories for us all, be-came a place to behold but forbidden to approach.

[Page 11]

The Pool

The pool was the third attraction. It was situated behind the river " Vershoky" not far from the Adamovitz farm. It was not visible from afar since it was surrounded by high banks. There was also a legend connected to the pool. During the Polish revolt against the Russians, a group of Polish rebels fled from a Cossack battalion. The Poles reached the pool and decided to throw in their money box and ammunition, swords, hand grenades etc. Some say they even threw in a cannon to avoid it being captured by the hateful Russians. The Poles then fled and scattered and thus no spoils were found by the Cossacks.

During the summer, when the pool dried up almost completely and only frogs populated its bottom, we would go there despite the danger of the ranch dogs, and search among the bushes for the lost treasure or the ammunition. Despite repeated disappointments, we never stopped visiting the pool, looking down its clear water and listening to the frogs croak, as this was the only pool nearby.

[Page 12]

Eishishok the town of Torah and Learners

M. Tzinowitz

Of all the towns in Lithuania, Zamut and White Russia, where Pharisee congregations existed, our town was renowned for its congregation of the best Yeshiva students some of whom later became Gaonim, and for the large numbers of students studying in the two Yeshivas, the " old" and the " new". The townsmen were distinguished for their love of the Torah and respect for its students. The Rabbis of the town were Talmudic scholars distinguished for their acumen in the Gemara, Posekim and Tosaphat as well as in practical teaching. They were of great service to the Yeshiva students studying to be teachers. Hence the attraction of the town.

The elders of Eishishok claim that the founder of the congregation of Pharisees in our town was a renowned righteous Rabbi named Rabbi Moshe. The following story about him was told: "On stormy, snowy Saturday night, Rabbi Moshe was not to be found among the students in the synagogue. When the janitor came at dawn, He found the Rabbi standing outside the door to prevent it from blowing open so that no chill should disturb the Torah students. Since the lock had broken and there had been no time to repair the door, the Rabbi spent the stormy night guarding the door with his own body - those inside had not noticed anything.

We may assume that this Rabbi Moshe was Rabbi Moshe Berabibi (son of) Aharon Halevi Horwitz, an Eishishok teacher in the time of Hagra, and one of the three Rabbis in Lithuania called upon to decide in the controversy of the Vilna Congregation, between Rabbi Shmuel Berabbi (son of) Avigdor the last President of the Court in the Vilna congregation and his congregation.

Eventually, a bigger and more elegant synagogue was erected and more Pharisees came to town.

In those days, approximately 150 years ago, the President of the Court in the town, was the famous Rabbi Yosele of Lipnishok, one of the best students of Rabbi Haim of Nalozia. He supported the Pharisee students in the town and was an example of Rabbinical authority.

At that time, Eishishok was famous for its Biblical expanders and the Pharisees had an opportunity to study this Rabbinical task. Thus, in 5574 (1814), Rabbi Yom-Tov Lipman, son of the Vilna Rabbinical teacher Rabbi Moshe Shlomo, was an active Rabbinical teacher. His book, " Kerod Yom Tov" (Honour of Holiday), on all the weekly portions (Sdarot) of the Pentateuch, met with the Approval of all the Lithuanian Scholars of the period, among them the author of " A Human Life". In later years, the renowned preacher Rabbi Itzhak of Vilkomir, the author of many books on Biblical exposition widely read in all Jewish communities in Lithuania, Zamut and White Russia, was an active expositor and preacher. Rabbi Idla of Volozin called him " the little Alshich" and the author of " Pithai Teshuva" (Gates of Repentance) referred to his novelties in the Aggadah as "faithful to the Torah". He spent the latter years of his life in Jerusalem and lived to be over 100.

The "Golden Era" of the Eishishok Pharisees was during the service of Rabbi Abraham Shmuel (5607-5615; 1847-1855), student of Rabbi David Teveli of Minsk and Rabbi Alexander Ziskind of Novoorodok. He was called the Great Gaon by Rabbis of the time and indeed, his excellent book " Pillars of Fire" published after his death, testifies to his greatness.

Rabbi Abraham Shmuel was also famous- for his righteousness, his deeds, and his noble character. He was sickly from youth and also very poor. Some large. communities asked him to honour them by residing with them but he rejected these offers since he wished to remain in Eishishok, the town of Torah, There he died in 5529 (1859) ,, He had served for a few years as president of court in Reisen in Zumyt but then returned to Eishishok where he died.

In the book "Ahavat David" the Love of David we read these, words of appreciation for this great man: "He never ate unless a guest joined his table₂ big law was law of truth and all was based on moderation and observation."

Of the rabbis in the town who exerted much influence on the Pharisees, one must note Rabbi Ben-Zion Sheternfeld, whose talmudic composition " Shaarei-Zedek" (Gates of Justice) is well-known in the Rabbinical and Yeshiva world. He was an advocate of traditional education and his great pamphlet "The Way of the Torah" which is a sharp reaction to the new system of education and the method of learning a summary of the main principles of the Torah, made a strong impression. The author of " Chofetz Haim" appreciated him greatly and adorned his own first compositions with Rabbi Shternfeld's approval. Notable among the later Eishishok rabbis is Rabbi Zvi Hirsch Ma -Yafit, a very clever man who held public office. He later became president of Court of the Volkoviski community of the Shavli district. Also notable was Rabbi Joseph Zundel Hutner, former rabbi of Deretshin, considered one of the great Lithuanian rabbis of the era and whose important compositions on all parts of the Shulchan-Aruch made him famous.

Some famous "Gaonim" spent time in Eishishok as "Pharisees". After studying in the Yeshivas of Volozin and Mir, some of these then made Eishishok the center for their studies. For some, Eishishok served as their only center beside their home towns. Of these we should note Rabbi Meir Simcha Hacohen author of "Or Sameach" (Happy Light), president of the court of Dvinsk, Rabbi Moshe Denishevsky, author of " Beer Moshe" (The Well of Moses), president of the court of Deslovocoka and one of the founders of "Hamizrachi:, Rabbi Avraham Ben Haim Liv Tiktinsky and others.

One of the natives of Eishishok, Rabbi Meir wrote of his native town that if was " world famous as a great Torah Center, which attracted many great Torah scholars who later became Rabbis and leaders.

Other notables who studied as Pharisees in Eishishok are the learned Rabbi Mordechai Plungian, teacher of Talmud in the Vilna Yeshiva for rabbis, later chief proofreader in the famous publishing house of the widow and brother Romm and author of famous books on linguistics and Hebrew commentary.

With the establishment and development of the Kovna Yeshiva, the increase of Yeshivas in Lithuania and especially the development of the Talmudic of the Talmudic community of nearby Radon to a large and central Yeshiva, the importance of the Eishishok "Kibbutz" decreased. Yet, till the outbreak of World War I, Eishishok held a considerable collection of Pharisees.

When Eishishok was annexed to the Lithuanian state of Kovna in 5700 (1940), the Radun Yeshiva transferred to Eishishok which also served as an initial transit station for the Polish refugees, especially Torah students, who fled from the internal Jewish enemy, the Jewish Communists. The people of Eishishok headed by their last Rabbi, Rabbi Shimon Rozovsky, acted in accordance with the famous Eishishok tradition and did much to ease the suffering of the refugees.

When the Jewish communities in Poland, Lithuania and Russia were destroyed, Eishishok, was among them. In the spiritual history of Israel, Eishishok will symbolize glory and beauty. (Published in " Hazophe" no. 2437, 1846).

[Page 15]

From Letters to the Editor
Rabbi Meir Stalwitz,
may his memory be blessed
(the late rabbi of Zichron Moshe, Jerusalem)

If I should wish to depict my native town Eishishok, my whole life on this earth would not suffice for doing so. Who can be more familiar than myself with the town, its people, how great they were and how much they contributed to the world.

I know that great men, observant and Gaonim, renowned in all the world, studied as children in Eishishok. Eishishok was world famous as a Torah town, and from the time I have been aware, I remember the names of the learned great rabbis of Eishishok: the Gaon Rabbi Ben Zion of Bilsk, the Gaon Rabbi Elyakum of Grodna, the Gaon Rabbi Zvi Hirsch of Volkovisk, the Gaon Rabbi Zundel Hutner and the last Gaon Rabbi Shimon Rozovsky, may G-d avenge him!

....Many of the students of the town's Yeshiva later became great biblical scholars ... The homeowners of Eishishok boasted that in this aspect their town was superior to all the big towns. One great scholar once suggested to them that they dispatch envoys in all the world and thus increase their " kibbutz" and they could support an additional few hundred Pharisees, but they replied that they did not wish to share with others. After the Almighty had endowed them with wise hearts to support 100 Pharisees in great honour, they did not want to give their goodness to others.

How my heart aches now that these towns were ruined and the great scholars murdered, their blood shed for no reason. Why was the anger poured on them???

I do not know if ever there was such a time, and there is nothing left for us to do but turn to G-d, Judge of the World that He may do justice when He judges the whole world.

[Page 16]

Rabbi Avraham Berish Rosing

I am pleased that you wish to perpetuate the memory of Eishishok, since it was the first center of our holy Torah in the state of Lithuania. I am greateful that I had the privilege of studying there in my childhood in the company of great scholars. Many of those who studied there later became great and renowned scholars, I do know that the Gaon Rabbi Meir Simcha may his holy memory be "blessed, and the Gaon Rabbi Eli Haim Meizel, The Honourable president of the Court of Lodz, and the Gaon Rabbi Yonatan who was Rabbi and president of the court in Bialystok, and was called " Vilaavaar Elui" and the Gaon Rabbi Haim Ozer Grodzensky of Vilna and many others, learned in their childhood in Eishishok.

The rabbis who held rabbinical seats in Eishishok were famous in the Jewish world. Eighty years ago, the great Gaon Rabbi Avraham Shmuel, author of " Pillars of Fire" (Amudei Esh), was in Rabbinical service, followed by the great Gaon Rabbi Benzion Bilsker, the energetic author of several books of "Questions and Answers", followed by the energetic Rabbi Elyakum Grudrner who was followed by the great Rabbi Zvi Hirsch Ma Yafit who had great insight into worldly affairs. In the days I studied there, the great Gaon and righteous man was Rabbi Yosef Zundil Hutner, whose nights were as days and who was extremely sharp and knowledgeable in all aspects of the Torah. He was author of several books on the four parts of the " Shulchan Aruch" (The Prepared Table). He was brother in law to the righteous Gaon Rabbi Haim Liv Stwisker may his sacred memory be blessed, author of the Question and Answers" book " A Lion's Face". Father of the great Gaon Rabbi Meir Stolevitch, author of " From the House of Meir", formerly Rabbi in Heslevitch and later Rabbi in Zichron Moshe in Jerusalem,

Rabbi Avraham may his sacred memory be blessed, was a great expert in the Torah as well as being a very righteous man.

The excellent Rabbi Gaon Yohanan Zopovitch,Rabbi of Tiberias and formerly of the Lithuanian town Radzivilshky, was also a native of Eishishok. Also the famous preacher of Minsk, Rabbi Benjamin Minsker, was a native of Eishishok. And the righteous Gaon Rabbi Henoch Hacohen who taught Torah for over 40 years, was also Eishishok born; he fathered the following Gaonim Rabbis:

Rabbi Yoel Hacohen who was also dean of the rabbinical college in Vilna for nearly 40 years, and the Rabbi Gaon Aharon Shmidt, formerly Rabbi of the Vison Community in Lithuania and presently of the rabbinical society of the Hagra (Gaon Rabbi Eliyahu of Vilna) Yeshiva and preacher in the " Gemara Society" and the society of " Tiferet Bahurim". Also the " Gaon of Dvinsk" studied in Eishishok in his childhood as well as the Rabbi Gaon Avraham Kalmanovitch Honorable President of the court of Tiktin,

The Gabbais (managers or treasurers of the synagogue) who endeavored on behalf of the Yeshiva students were: in the old Yeshiva, Rabbi Avraham Openheim and his brother in law Rabbi Benjamin Ratner and in the new Yeshiva Rabbi Shlomo Drucker ("Ferber"), father of the Rabbi Gaon Yaakov, president of the court of Osstrin and author of "Proverbs of Wisdom" (Imrei Haskel) and other books. He was very knowledgeable in the Bible and an excellent expositor, intelligent as well as a very pleasant man.

The second Gabbai was also an excellent man of the distinguished lineage of Rabbi Baruch Eli, son of the Gaon Rabbi Menachem Mendel, the honorable president of the court of the Radun community.

The home owners in Eishishok were excellent people, G-d fearing and knowledgeable in the Torah and even the poorer ones supported the needs of the yeshiva students with great respect. Due to their respect for the Torah, they had the privilege of having rabbis as sons and sons in laws. Eishishok was the only community which did not send emissaries to the Diaspora communities since the homeowners shouldered the responsibility of supporting the Yeshiva students and donated considerable sums of this purpose, even beyond their means. Not only prosperous and middle class home owners participated in this effort; but also the artisans; coachmen, shoemakers, tailors, and other hard workers. It was a great pleasure for them to support the "Pharisees" and they treated the students as loyal fathers treat only sons. Happy is the eye which beheld all this! And how great is our sorrow that this large town of Israel and its dear inhabitants, worthy before G-d and their fellow men, were victims of evil men and that we have no remnants of this Torah center, mother of the largest Yeshivas in Lithuania.

Written by Rabbi Avraham Brish Rosing, founder of the "Tehilat Israel" society in the big synagogue in Tel-Aviv, Rabbi and president of the court in the Limberg community in Latvia, called " Ber Salanter" in Eishishok.

HaRav HaGaon, R' Yosef Zundel Hutner, one of the great geniuses of his time. Served as Chief Rabbi of Eishishok for 25 years (the picture is on a German identity card from 1916 - two years before his death, and he was then about 71 years old)

HaRav HaGaon, R' Shimon Rozovski hy"d - the last Rabbi of
Eishishok (see page 125)

[Page 18]

[Page 18]

From the Press of the Period;
Hashachar (The Dawn)
4th copy, 1879; by Yaapaz, written in 1878

Eishishok is a small town with lots of people, one of the worst towns in Lithuania. It has three crooked streets. Its market is very wide, equaling in width its length, and at its center there is a circle of 30 shops, which have turned green with age. The elders believe that demons dance there at night. The shops are as small as chicken pens, they have side-entrances and it is no small difficulty to enter them. The turnover is small since there are more shops than buyers, Thursday is market day and then the air is filled with the quarrels of old ladies. They are surrounded by stacks of barley bread and cakes as black as raven wings. These are bought only when someone is ill because otherwise people bake for themselves. The noise and curses here remind one of Yatkaaiva street in Vilna, In 1865 the whole town was burnt down, and only the circle of shops, the end of Vilna street and the " old" Yeshiva remained. The houses are dilapidated, the streets unpaved and dirty. The women are occupied chiefly with washing clothes while their husbands roam the villages to make a living. The two Yeshivas and a synagogue form a triangle. They are surrounded with stables, a toilet house and not for the cemetery.

There are about 80 " Pharisees" studying in the two Yeshivas. One man, Haim " Treger", brings food to the Yeshiva for 10 kopeks a week from each Pharisee. In the old Yeshiva, the food carrier is Gedalya Shekradz. Ropes are tied round his back and these are beaded with pottery and mugs. Gedalya goes from door to door to collect cheese, milk and herring for the Pharisees. In the old days when the inherited land still belonged to the Eishishok Jews, Gedalya was a cow herd.

Each year a Rabbi would come to test the Pharisees in the laws of Tfilah and Niddah (non kosher food and impurity) and for 5 RO he would give them rabbinical ordination. But because of lack of rabbinical seats most were forced to become teachers and remained bitterly poor.

The town had three butchers, two shames and two permanent Dayanim. The new Yeshiva had four Gabbais, the baker - an old sinner who harassed the learned, - a repentant who afflicted himself and was as dangerous as "a bear robbed of its cubs", The second Gabbai, Shalom Gershon G,harassed the Haskalah lovers. The third-, Bitz - was as hypocritical as Lava'n the Aremite. The fourth-Yehuda K. a commoner from a family of wagoners- was a cheat and a thief.

Their righteous rabbi issued a decree forbidding the acceptance of bachelors to the Pharisee community but when the numbers of those joining the community decreased, the decree was cancelled and as a result the numbers of boys who came increased, among which were many Haskalah lovers. At the point, the fanatics began persecuting the latter and one yeshiva boy, son of a famous rabbi, was expelled in disgrace. Letters were written to his home town accusing him of scepticism and he was tormented on this account. In the month of Elul, the synagogue treasurers and the fanatics convened and decided that those who handed over their heretic books to be burned and signed in the book that they would turn their back on their evil ways, would not be harmed. Many of the soft hearted succumbed and turned over their books to the fanatics. But other Haskalah lovers continued to pore over their books in secret until an informant made the practice known. Arie, the baker, turned heaven and earth till at last it was decided to burn the books in public and this was done. One boy was found to have an edition of " Hashachar" (The Dawn) and the town was in uproar but he could not be expelled since he supported himself.

The Gabbais invaded the Pharisee rooms, broke locks and carried away books by Shulman, Smolenskin, "The Sins of Youth", "Love of Zion" to the rabbis' house where they were burned.

In the summer of 5637(1877) a bookseller came to town with Haskalah books most of which he had in the hotel. Judge Rabbi ben Yehoshua wrote the hotel owner to hand over the heretic books to Gabbai Shalom Gershon and pawn them till the bookseller left Eishishok so that he would be unable to sell them to the Pharisees and influence them.

(The above letter is presented in its entirety though some matters mentioned are vastly exaggerated. We can learn however of matters concerning earlier generations which the author mentions incidentally, It is an irrefutable fact that Eishishok, supposedly so dark and obscure, produced many authors and learned men who honorably represented their home town , the town of Torah and Pharisees, signed, The Editors,)

[Page 20]

From the Memoirs of A.A. Friedman
5686 (1926) Tel Aviv

Mr. Friedman was formerly Warsaw Editor of Hatzopheh

Eishishok is an old, worn-out town, Its streets are covered knee-high with mud. Its houses are decrepit wooden structures and its Jewish inhabitants are bent and broken. Their whole life is concentrated on the worries of making a living, petty minded details of their trade and low pay.

But their deep black eyes also transmit feeling of pride, This pride is due to their being inhabitants of Eishishok which is a center of Torah in Lithuania, second to the nearby Volozhin. The Yeshivas are full of all kinds of students from near and far. All studiously pore over the Torah while the townsmen provide them with bread and stews and some of the fanatic Orthodox home owners conduct the whole business. Some of these are hypocrites who furiously persecute any student found with a suspect book. In such cases they invade the students' sleeping quarters and search through their belongings. Any "unkosher" book is confiscated. At times, following a general search, they conduct an auto-da-fe in the synagogue court. I myself witnessed how a book found in the quarters of Pharisee was brought to one Gabbai but the title page had been torn off. Students did this several times in order to prevent suspicion. On the first page of that book a dedication had been written. The dedication began with capitalized letters reading "El Kavod". The "learned" mistook these words for the title of a famous banned book and triumphantly ordered it burned.

One tall man whose face was roughly lined was pointed out to me. His name was Todros and the following legend was told about him: when he was a baby, his parents gave him to the care of a wet-nurse, as was the general practice in Lithuania, His parents later took him from the first wet-nurse and transferred him to another. The first lady issued a legal claim to the court in the town and later transferred the claim to a higher court. The baby had meanwhile spent two years with the second wet-nurse and eventually reached the age of Bar-Mitzvah, marriage and good deeds. When Todros was 30 years old, the court finally issued an order that he be treated by the first wet nurse... who by that time was an old woman. Hence the Lithuanian proverb, "Todros must suck" which is said to express dissatisfaction when settling a matter is delayed for a long time.

[Page 22]

The Great Fire of 1895

One of the major events in Eishishok was the great fire of 1895, Most of the houses in the town, which were built of wood, were destroyed in this fire. Also the Yeshiva schools were burned. After the fire, the dates of event in Eishishok such as births and weddings were calculated as of the "great fire", The big register of the burial society which was several hundred years old, was also destroyed.

The fire received wide coverage in the Hebrew press of the time, Rabinovitz, the editor of "Hamelitz" and author A.L. Levinsky, both former Eishishok yeshiva students, wrote several articles on the subject. It is interesting to note that Levinsky and other writers emphasized the fact that the homeowners had themselves supported the yeshiva and its hundreds of Pharisees and did not turn for help from the outside as was the practice of the other famous yeshivas of the time, Volozhin, Novogrodek and others. There is therefore, these writers claim, a double duty to help reconstruct and generously support the Torah-town.

A special committee was formed under the patronage of the district governor, which collected contributions for the town.

We now bring excerpts from "Hamelitz" newspaper and the book of the Dayyan Rabbi Elazar (Rabbi Layzar) Vilkansky, The Jews of the village were responsible for reconstructing not only the ruins of their village but also the center of Torah learning. The yeshiva schools were slowly built and Pharisee students again began to flock there. The Eishishok Jews, despite their own financial distress, welcomed them hospitably and shared with them their bread. Their main concern was the scarcity of books many of which had been destroyed by the fire, An article published in the newspaper " Hatzfira" a year after the fire, testifies to this need, In this article, Mendel Itzhak Berman appeals on behalf of the committee of Hatzfira readers, for contributions of books to the yeshiva schools in the town for Eishishok to become once again a center of learning. He writes that the treasury of the yeshiva is empty and there still remain outstanding bills for the yeshivas burned in the fire. Contributors names, he promises, will be immortalized in the register of the community,

[Page 23]

Hamelitz
(24 Sevan, 5655-June 4, 1895)

Three weeks have passed since G-d's anger was poured upon the Jewish towns and newspapers are full of terrible descriptions of the state of these towns and their unhappy inhabitants. It is wondrous that among the other burned towns, the forsaken Eishishok is mentioned only in passing. ..." the child will not cry and its nurse will not rush to its aid" ....Eishishok is silent and no one takes it to heart, Indeed, the town has been silent thus far...shocked into silence since the disaster is unbearable. 400 houses were destroyed and the few whose houses were spared, lost their money and property to the destitute who saved nothing. Thus all the town's residents are wretched together.

Eishishok is situated far from a city, the business of the town was concentrated in the town itself and the residents made their living off each other. The fire left them naked and therefore the disaster is so great and intolerable,

Please be merciful, generous Jews, and have compassion for the 3000 destitute people now tramping the streets and fields, hungry and naked, with no support and nothing to lean on. Remember how Eishishok has served as a center for Torah learning and has never depended on outside assistance. Support it now as it is so very poor.

[Page 24]

The Fires and the Burned
(Hamelitz-20 Tamuz, 5655; June30, 1895)

A.L.Levinsky

Had Eishishok been the only town burned, there would be hope for its reconstruction, But Eishishok has no luck even in burning. It was burned just when Brisk, Kobrin and others were also burned, This makes everyone think: what is Eishishok in comparison with Brisk? Only a native of a small town who realizes what ruin a fire can cause to such a small town, will understand the situation of Brisk and Eishishok,

In Eishishok no Jew can earn a decent sum of money in one year to enable him to build himself a house - so who would take the trouble of rebuilding the ruined town? But Eishishok is not a town to be compared with other small towns, Eishishok is extraordinary. It is a center of Torah learning in the full sense. It cannot be compared even to Volozhin, Volozhin lives off its student guests, its Torah is of Israel and its living if off its Torah. Eishishok in contrast, supported its Torah center not for the sake of a reward, and indeed, it supported a fine Torah Center, All its guests were satisfied and earned their bread honorably.

In my childhood I heard wonders about Eishishok's love of the Torah and its Pharisee students who were supported by the natives themselves, the natives would rather go hungry and thirsty so long as the students would suffer no want. Those who study before G-d will not want for bread or water; there will always be a candle to provide light and wood to keep them warm, the good people of the town supplied everything - they never asked for charity, nor did they send out emissaries, nor did they negotiate nor make a big fuss. This small town often supported 500 students. And this town was burned.

We have an obligation to honour and rebuild it. Eishishok never asked the holy congregation of students for anything and preferred to support the Torah itself and this involved supporting perhaps myriads of our brothers. Now the town is burned, we all have a responsibility to support the survivors, May they rebuild their homes and the center of Torah studies!

[Page 25]

Hamelitz-September 14, 1896

Four months have passed since our town-center of Torah studies has voiced its appeal for the mercy of our merciful brothers. Chaos and destruction are still wide- spread. More than anything else, we are concerned about the yeshiva schools while we, residents of Eishishok, can in no way completely rebuild ourselves...Well-known Gaonim came from our town, For approximately 100 years the Eishishok schools provided education and when the Volozhin yeshiva was destroyed, Eishishok remained alone. Eishishok has not healed from its heartbreaking misfortune even after the contribuitons it received. Where shall Eishishok look for help if it cannot depend on those pure-hearted people cpable of appreciating its qualities and importance?

We must conclude with the following announcement: our president of the court is moving to the town of Vilkavishk, We therefore request the honorable rabbis to avoid exerting themselves to come to Eishishok to apply for the vacancy since we will only summon and offer the rabbinical seat to a rabbi of our choice.

Speech of Haim son of Rabbi Moshe Strelitzky

Excerpt from the book "From Wave to Wave"

by Meir Vilkansky

It was market day and the town was full of Goyim and carts. When the fire broke pit everyone tried to escape from the town, pushing through the pedestrians...The fire leapt from roof to roof... it suddenly appeared in unexpected places...The fire spread throughout the town, women and children were rushing through clouds of dust and flames of fire., the whole town became one great flame...the people fled to the grass banks of the river and crouched there or rushed about. A howl arose from the crowd for the babies and holy books burned in the fire. Children and hid from the fire beneath the bench in the " Heder" and there burned alive. My niece was burned in her crib. Her father came running home from his shop; he shouted out to find out of anyone was at home and no one answered; he grabbed a pillow in his hand and fled. Woe! He did not look in the crib! The pillow was saved and the baby burned....

People were pushing along the river and through the fields frantically searching for lost ones...the day was ending ,,,the fire receded, but the sky was red and enflamed. ..when dawn broke the city had vanished from the face of the earth.,,only a group of houses.in the " new street" (Radun St.) survived, This was due to the trees in the Pharmacy garden which blocked the fire and arrested its advance, The weeping did not cease.,, people searched for burned bodies... seven mothers were howling beside the bones of their children burned in the heder and the sound of their cries rose to the skies, the ruins of the two yeshivas and the synagogue stood naked.

Days passed. Carts loaded with bread and clothes came from nearby towns. Money was also sent. The editor of " Hamelitz" sent 3 rubles for the survivors and published an article and a call for support for this town which had always provided support for its yeshiva students. He neither took vengeance nor bore a grudge, He forgot how Eishishok had expelled him in shame from the yeshiva and the town (after being caught reading Haskalah books - the editor).

[Page 27]

The Zionist Movement in Eisiskes

The Zionist Organization of Eishishok

Rumours of Dr. Herzl's appearance and the first Zionist congress reached even remote Eishishok (70 km. away form the district town Vilna), On the initiative of the eldest son of Rabbi Eliezer the Judge, Itzhak Vilkansky (now Prof, Itzhak Volkani, head of the Institute for Agricultural Research in Rehovot) a meeting of the town's " Maskilim," readers of " Hamelitz" and "Hatsfira" was held. These people were painfully aware of the distress of the Jewish people and yearned for liberation. The Zionist idea was fiercely opposed by the Orthodox and extremist "homeowners" who, like the orthodox everywhere, viewed Zionism as a danger to religion and opposed " the anticipation of the coming of the Messiah supported by the western atheists and the eastern enlightened, A few young people did however, master enough courage in the compressed extremist Pharisee atmosphere of Eishishok at that time, to lay the foundation of the Zionist organization. It is interesting to note that these early and few Zionists received enthusiastic support from the simple naive warm hearted and straight minded crafsmen.

These people flocked to the Zionist meetings, "drinking in" with belief and enthusiasm the lofty and wonderful words of Jewish revival, a Jewish state and great leader Dr. Hertzel,

Meir Vilkansky, the youngest son of Rabbi Laiser the Judge (known in Israel by his literary name M. Elazari) describes in his book " From Wave to Wave" the formation and early days of the Zionist Organization in Eishishok:

"…This is what my brother did upon his second returning from the place of Torah, He went whispering with some of his friends to the tavern of Yaakov Setzkin, the American (fictitious name - the editor). There they decorated the walls with pictures and hung a bright lamp from the ceiling. In the rear they arranged a table with books and spy books. That evening my brother stood at the head of the table and in the lamplight announced to the people the plans for a Jewish State in Israel.

A Jewish man has arisen by the name of Dr. Herzl, who will redeem his people, bring them to their country and create a state for them. A license will be obtained.

He did not spread his arms in the manner of a preacher to the Holy Ark and the people. His head was bowed, his hands grasped the table and in his suppressed voice seemed to be talking more to himself. But his face was flushed and his voice quivered. Also other faces became flushed and other hearts were struck. In this enthusiasm the Zionist organization was founded.

Again the platform was taken by a speaker. Not a fortune-teller but a preacher sent by the regional Zionist center. Each preacher was directed to adapt his words to the spirit of each town. This preacher stood in his Tallith before the Holy Ark. The Yeshiva was completely full. Zionist youths and Zionist artisans came; also other Jews who wanted to hear of Israel's plight and redemption attended. A long table was placed at the entrance so that everyone would buy a shekel and a share after the preacher concluded. (the shekel was the annual membership fee of the Zionist organization).

The home owners and really Orthodox did not attend. They timed their entrance exactly for the beginning of the Maariv prayer. But the prayer was delayed due to the preacher's sermon.

The hall was vibrant with the fiery words which captured the hearts and that evening the Maariv prayer was as fervently recited as on Yom Kippur eve. The crowd pressed upon the table at the entrance of the Yeshiva, The deep bowl filled with coins for the settlement of Israel and Reb Avraham Haneeman, who had also prayed close to the door, approached the table and cried " Give me a Shekel"!

My town divided, while all the wealthy objected, the young were attracted and the artisans enthused, Shlomo the tailor preached in the tailors minyan, Abba the shoemaker, preached in the shoemakers Minyan, They bought shekels and shares, They cried, " We shall rise and succeed!"

The Zionist organization in Eishishok was founded by Itzhak Vilkansky in 1897, after the first Zionist congress, Those chosen to the first committee were:

Reb Tuvia Rubinstein (known as " Darr Yeremitsher), Yehoshua Slovotsky, Yehuda Yaakov Snitzky, Zvi Levzovesky, may he long live (now- residing in Petach-Tikva), Zvi Levzovesky, Itzhak Vilkansky and myself. The heart and soul of the committee and society was Itzhak Vilkansky who served as secretary. When he went abroad to study, Shmuel Senitzky took his place. As was usually the case, in those first years of political Zionism, activities were limited to selling shekels and shares of the Colonial Bank.

Sometimes preachers would come from the district town Vilna, Initially the attitude of most of the townsmen to Zionism was hostile and negative. The Orthodox tried to besmirch us and accuse us falsely of being "anticipators of the Messiah" and atheists. But a large portion of the younger homeowners and most artisans supported us and so the fanatics battle against us did not succeed. One example of the Zionist enthusiasm in Eishishok at the time is that 140 shares of the Zionist bank were sold; as the price of a single share was 10 rubles, this was a very considerable sum for an Eishishok Jew.

When the fanatics saw our success, they tried to recruit the Gaon " HaChofetz Haim" whom they brought to preach against the Zionists. But all their efforts were in vain. The town's rabbi, Zundil Hutner, who spent his days and nights studying the Torah and working, did not persecute us. As a gentle hearted man, he avoided fights all his life. It was typical of him to reply to Meir Shalom Dubitsky, who came to ask whether, as an Orthodox Jew he is permitted to buy a shekel, that that is no sin according to the Torah.

Thus many Torah and yeshiva students joined our society, Besides the Zionist society, another society was founded. The speakers there were Rabbi Paltiel, Zvi Levzovesky and in particular Joshua Slovotzky, Members of the Zionist organization were only men - Eishishok was too Pharisee fanatical to allow the membership of women, But in our practical work we were at times assisted by women,

In the Minsk conference of Russian Zionists (1902) our representative was the lawyer Snitzky. When the teacher Archimovitz, brother in law of Leib Rudzin, came to town, the society of "Poalei Zion" (workers of Zion) was founded, During the years of 1904-1905 also a Bund party existed which attracted the working youth of the town, The Bund was then at the height of its activities and its influence was great while ours decreased slightly. The conflict between the Zionists and the Bund concentrated mainly on the conquest of the municipal library which was the only one in town.

At a later period, close to the First World War, Raphael Nahimovitz and Botvinik were chiefly active in Zionist matters.

When "modern heders" were extablished in Lithuania, we decided to extablish one also in Eishishok. We invited Mr. Archimovitz to be the teacher. When the Orthodox found out, they raised hell and loudly warned of the danger to Judaism. They convened, preached in public and nearly excommunicated us. When they realized how strongly we desired to open a "modern heder" ("dangerous heder" is what they called it) and that pupils had already registered, they rushed the Gaon Chofetz Haim from nearby Radun to influence us to cancel our evil and dangerous plan.

Rabbi Israel Meir came. Meir Kyuchevsky and myself were called upon to see him and he began to appeal to us to cancel our plan. When he saw our resistance, he burst into tears. This affected Meir Kyuchevsky who promised to withdraw but I was stubborn. The " modern heder" was established to the horror of the fanatics and it became a fact. It operated intermittently in various apartments till the establishment of the modern Hebrew school after World War I.

[Page 31]

The Society for " Hebrew Only"
Rak Ivrit

Eishishok's very special activity was the teaching of Hebrew to children. On the initiative of Sara Vilkansky (now- living in Raanana), daughter of the Judge, Rabbi Leiser, a society was established in 1905/6 in Eishishok by the name of "Hebrew Only." Students were girls from the age of six and up. The main duty of these "members" was to talk only Hebrew among themselves. For each word spoken not in Hebrew they were fined one kopek (an agura), which was given to the society's treasury. Each evening the girls would get together and the tutor Sara (who was replaced after her Aliyah, by her sisters Esther and Lea, may they rest in peace) would read the girls stories, tell them about Israel and the Zionist organization and teach them the few national songs then circulating ("Hatikva", " Where the Cedars Grow", " Hurry Brothers, Hurry" and others). From time to time, public "parties" were organized for parents and relatives and the girls would present small plays, declaim and sing in chorus and so on. This society was the foundation of the Hebrew movement in the town and due to its influence, the Hebrew language became common usage till the end.

The First World War brought a temporary cessation to the activities of this society. Immediately upon the establishment of a routine of life under German occupation, the "Hebrew Only" society resumed its activities. Sara Rubinstein, daughter of Reb Tuvia ("Der Yerementser") who was herself a member of the society in her childhood, returned to Eishishok and began reestablishing the society. About a year later, she was joined by Shaul Kaleko who also came to Eishishok and began working on spreading the Hebrew language. The society grew and embraced nearly all of the learning youth in the town. The new society of Hebrew speakers by the name of " Hauerkaz" (The Center) was founded for older youth, A club was opened (in the house of Eliyahu Bastunsky) where nearly all the young people convened each evening to spend their free time reading newspapers, playing and attending lectures on Zionist and literary subjects.

[Page 32]

Zionist Youth Movements

After the First World War, the younger generation became predominant in Zionist activities. In 1920, a Poalei Zion party was founded in Eishishok on the initiative of Shaul Kaleko and with the active participation of the young Paikovsky and Dembrovsky. " Poalei Zion" embraced the great majority of the labor youth of the town and the "unrestrained" yeshiva boys. But the party did not last long - when the active members left Eishishok it fell apart and was succeeded by the various Zionist youth movements.

During the years 1919-1920 the youth society " Cherut Vetehiya" (Freedom Revival) was active. Its participants were most of the "homeowners" in the town. This society was headed by Shalom Sonenson, Shaul Shneider, Rachel and Peretz Kaleko, Zeev Kaganovitz, Mordechai Levsovsky, Shlomo Kyuchevsky and others. For youngsters 10-14 years of age, there was the society " Pirchai Zion" (Flowers of Zion) and during 1922 - 1923 the club in the memory of Brener founded by S, Shneider and P. Kaleko, in 1924, the latter two founded the " Hashomer Hatzair" organization, which existed until 1939.

During 1925-1926, with the increase of immigration to Eretz Israel, the Zionist movement reached the height of its activity and success. Immigration was instigated during the rule of the Polish minister Grevesky, notorious for his behavior to Polish Jewry. The pressure of heavy taxes and other economic persecution imposed by the Grevesky rule, with the aim of "liberating "Poland of its large Jewish population, resulted in the immigration of many to Israel - "the fourth Aliyah". In each city, "Hachalutz" organizations were founded.

In Eishishok an organization of "Hachalutz Hamizrachi" was first established by Yoseph Reznick, Pesach Kopelenski, Fruma Rachel Ratz, Peretz Kaleko, Zipporah Lovetzky and with the assistance of N, Radunsky and Munin who were members of the " Hachalutz Hamizrachi "center in Vilna,

The "Hachalutz Hamizrachi" organization numbered more than 100 members from various circles not necessarily Orthodox and during its two years of existence was very active in providing information on Zionism and Pioneering as well as in training people for Aliya. And many members did indeed make "Aliyah" to Israel. The "Hachalutz Haklali" was founded two years later by Uri Rozovsky and Simcha Kaleko. As the saying goes, "jealousy among scholars will increase knowledge"; indeed, a very lively competition existed between the two parties with fertile results: numerous meetings, conferences, parties and balls were held and public life was very active.

Garden plots were leased by the two parties so that their members, all of whom were candidates for Aliya, should undergo a practical course in agriculture to train them for work in Israel. On the streets of the town one could often see pioneers striding on foot or sitting on carts filled with hay, big sickles in their hands or on their shoulders and their young, sweating faces beaming with triumph and pleasure.

The dream of all these youths was to obtain an immigration permit to Israel. The lucky few were escorted by their friends and the townsmen irrespective of party affiliation; parties and processions were held, wild hora was danced and fiery speeches were made by the renowned "brave mouths" of the town.

The few anti-Zionists, remnants of the Bund and the communists, vanished from public life and were not heard from. They dared not appear in public because the general atmosphere was Hebrew-Zionist. The artisans' children i.e., the lower and working classes, filled the ranks of the youth Zionist organizations. Also the economic organizations: the merchant union and the artisan union, were dominated by Zionists and no one objected.

When the Beitar organization appeared in the Zionist world, a strong Beitar unit was also formed in Eishishok. At a later period, also a Zionist Revisionist organization was established in the town, Both organizations reached the peak of their activity during the last years prior to World War II and were headed by Shlomo Kyuchevsky, Meir Shimon Politzky, Dov Shlipek and others.

Cultural life also flourished, The Hebrew school was growing despite its many difficulties. Plays in Hebrew and Yiddish were held by local or outside actors. The young people saw no future in Poland and dreamt of Israel, waiting for the moment they could fulfill this dream and live a free life in Israel,

And then came the terrible Holocaust which brought an end to the dreamers and their dreams.

[Page 34]

The Library and Amateur Theatre

The public Library was founded when the Zionist movement first came to Eishishok, During World War I when most of the well to do and active townsmen left for Vilna (in the end of the summer of 1915) in dread of the Russian Cossacks, the library was almost completely destroyed.

After Eishishok was captured by the Germans in 1915, most of the refugees, including many Jews, returned to the town. As is known, also the Nazi's ancestors were not overly affectionate to the Jews but it must be noted to their credit, that they hardly intervened in the social and cultural life,

At that period, Eishishok was very fortunate in its leader. Reb Meir Kyuchevsky, an enlightened and clever man of action with a profound social sense, He won the trust of the Germans and therefore succeeded in re-establishing a normal and public life in the town. On his initiative, a "comitat" was founded whose main purpose was to supervise the just distribution of the portions of bread and wheat the Germans administered, as well as the clothing which later began to arrive from the U.S. for the Jews.

A soup-kitchen for the poor was also established. The vital spirit in the "comitat" and the executor of ths decisions was young Shmuel Kaleko, may G-d avenge his blood. He concentrated all activities and was its representative before the local and outside charitable committees.

Since he also loved books, he began, when first returning from Vilna, to devote time and effort to reorganizing the destroyed public library. He and Benjamin Chorny went from house to house to collect the few remnant books of the old library which were to form the foundation of a new one. Actually, the library was at that time a basic "necessity of life; the Germans had imposed a curfew after 7 p.m. so the young people were confined to their homes every evening. In such a situation, what better pastime than reading could they have?

Efforts were made to expand the library by donations of books and money, lotteries etc. Nevertheless, the limited numbers of books could not satisfy the hunger of the increasing number of readers. A big operation to purchase more books was then launched by staging plays the proceed of which were used for that purpose.

Sara Pinon the teacher (who was not a native of Eishishok) organized a drama group which staged the well known play of Gordin, "Hassia De Yethoma".

The customary theatre, stage and curtain were set up in the stable of Arie Leib, the horse merchant, on Radun St. All the work involved in arranging the stage, the benches etc. was of course, done voluntarily by theatre and library supporters.

One most note to the Germans' credit that they generously supported this project both in providing the necessary materials and purchasing expensive tickets,

The dramatic group consisted of Fruma Rachel Katz, Shmuel Haim Gross, Shaul Kaleko, '¦ Benjamin Chorny and later Yosef Michelovsky, Shin Katzenelboygen and others. When Sara Pinon left Eishishok, Shaul Kaleko took her place at the head of the group and he was later succeeded by Yosef Michelovsky. The plays of the Eishishok theatre were attended also by guests from nearby towns.

In 1918 the foundation was laid for a separate Hebrew library. With the increase of Hebrew readers as a result of the spreading of Hebrew by Zionist societies and evening classes, there was a corresponding increase in the demand for Hebrew books. As the general library was more concerned with the purchase of Yiddish books, a special play was staged (Der Inteligent by P. Hirshbin) the proceeds of which, amounting to several hundred German marks, were used to purchase Hebrew books.

Meir Kyuchevsky demanded that this money be contributed to poor people ill with typhus (at that time there was an epidemic of typhus in the town which killed about 100 people in one year), but the younger people objected strongly, claiming that care of the sickly poor was the duty of the community leaders, As is always the case, the people were divided on the issue but the matter ended well since Havale Strelitzky (now residing in Israel) who was representative of the young people, had already reached Vilna, bought books with the money and sent them to Eishishok, the elders felt compelled to leave it at that. Thus the peace was restored.

The public library, which later contained several thousand Hebrew and Yiddish books, played an important part in the public life of the youth, The library represented a strong " position" over which the Yiddishists and Hebrews fought through the years. The amateur acting group continued to perform many and various plays, Later the youth societies also formed drama clubs which staged plays and playlets in Hebrew.

The committee of Eishishok' Youth Club named after Y. H. Brenner, 1923

The committee of *"HeHalutz Hatzair"* in Eishishok in the year 5685 (1925)

The Economic Situation

The Economic Situation

What were the occupations of the townspeople? In early days, the Eishishok Jews dealt mainly in commerce but many were farmers. The Jews owned wide fields reading far beyond the Virshoky River. But during the reign of Nicholai I, who was an oppressor of Jews, most of the fields were taken from the Jews and divided among the Goyim of the town. The latter built houses and planted trees as boundaries between their land and the land still remaining in Jewish hands. Thus the " Pigs Street" (Svinaga-Ulitsa), which surrounded the Jewish Streets on the west and north, was created.

The townspeople were related mainly to a few prominent families (Hashrovitzim, Shimshelevitz, Kabachnik and others) who owned most of the houses, fields and gardens on the west and south sides. The vegetable gardens were planted with potatoes, cucumbers, beets, carrots and more, the produce of which not only answered to all the Jews' needs all year round but also left a considerable surplus to be sold on market days. Most homeowners also owned cows and goats which grazed in the public pasture near the village, "Dumbliya". Attempts were constantly made by the village Goys to rob the Jews of this pasture and thus began a large series of trials which lasted dozens years and which were alternately settled in favor of the Jews and the Goys. These trials drained the public treasury but the Jews were unwilling to surrender the Jewish remnants of the many lands once belonging to them.

Only when the Polish rule began, did the Polish townsmen get a settlement in their favor and all this land was transferred to their ownership. The Jewish community then leased another pasture-land on the community's name, by the water mill on Mill Road, and there the Jewish cows grazed without disturbance.

The Jews were also occupied with shopkeeping, peddling and horse and hide dealing. At the center of the town, a row of fancy goods and fabric shops was located. (Ryad-Kraman) . These shops turned into the general market on their eastern side and faced the horse-market on the west where iron and paint shops were located. At the northern and southern sides, shops were located.

Market day was on Thursday which was also the redemption day. All the shopkeepers and artisans, such as hat-makers, blacksmiths, bakers, greengrocers, fabric dealers whose livelihood depended on the Goyim, looked forward to this day. Hundreds of peasant carts came from all over the vicinity and filled the market square and adjacent alleys. All week long the town lived off the redemptions of this day. On Friday, the shopkeepers and artisans collected their debts and settled their accounts.

On other workdays, except for Sunday, one rarely saw a Goy in the market and if by chance one appeared, all the shopkeepers pounced on him and attempted to persuade him to enter their respective shops by spinning stories of unmatchable bargains or even by actually pulling him by the hand or button hole. Four times a year a fair was held which attracted merchants also from other districts, especially horse and pig merchants as well as several horse-thieves.

The town also had big tanneries most of which belonged to the " Kabachnikim" where cheap and plain leather was tanned for the peasants and softer leather for the Jews. The tanneries also sent leather to the city. Merchandise needed by the shopkeepers and artisans was brought by coachmen from the city. Sunday morning, 12-15 coaches would leave for the district city of Vilna, filled with sacks and merchants sitting on them containing the produce of Eishishok: leathers, geese, chicken, flax, pigs-bristles, etc.

Wednesday afternoon the coaches returned stacked with city goods for market day. Wednesday evening was a sleepless night of hard work organizing the merchandise on shelves, preparing boxes etc.

At the end of the 19th century an actual factory existed in Eishishok, This was the match factory of Joseph Stelevitz which worked for several decades; it employed 100 workers, mainly women and thus supported many families and provided dowries for the girls.

Initially, the matches were lighted by striking a wall or shoe-sole. Later the modern matches, lighted by striking the coating of their box, were produced.

When the Russian government imposed a tax on matches, so high that it comprised 50% of the income, the factory could no longer support itself and was closed.

An " alms box" was founded to assist the poor shopkeepers and artisans. They could borrow a few rubles without interest by pawning goods. A public sick fund was also founded.

The " alms box" was handled by Reb Eliyahu Dumblyanski, It was a private box yet he did not profit from it. He lent everyone small sums and received a pawn on the loan. He would wait several years for repayment and only after giving numerous notices, would he sell the pawned objects at a public auction.

When he died, at 105 years of age it is said, his alms box stopped operating.

This was not the case with the sick fund which supported the sickly poor of the town. Also this fund was founded on the initiative of one person, Reb Benjamin of the Kaganovitz family, called " Benjamin Der Kapalyushik" by the townspeople. He carried the treasury box in a little bag round his neck. The money was put in special boxes by Jewish women before candle lighting on Shabbath and holidays.

Twice a year Reb Benjamin would come round to empty the contents and thus the funds increased. The trustees of the treasury were Reb Moshe Streletzky who was succeeded by Reb Meir Shalom Dubitzky and others.

In 1909 a bank was founded on the initiative of Reb Meir Kyuchevsky and Hershel Remz and also, may they live long, Reb Zeer Shneider and Zvi Levzovsky. Each member deposited a certain sum which formed the capital of the bank, New members joined and the capital increased. and later the bank received 2,000 rubles from J.C.A. (Jewish Colonization Association) and in 1914, its credit amounted to 15,000 rubles. Meir Seiritzky served as first secretary of the bank, followed by Michael Vilensky, may he rest in peace, whose successor for many years was Haim Mordechai Pacianko.

During the final ten years before Eishishok's destruction, several big economic enterprises were erected such as the flour mill and power station of the brothers Kyuchevsky, the latter of which provided the town with benefits of electric lighting. Economic organizations were also formed and these provided their members with financial and organizational aid and also promoted the development of the town.

First and foremost of the economic organizations was the merchants' union. This union was created in 1919 when the Polish government took over and most of the shopkeepers and merchants were members. The main cause for its formation was the hostile attitude of the Polish authorities to Jewish commerce and their desire to drive the Jews out of the business. To this end, they used taxes which were increased yearly and regulations of all sorts and kinds as to make life for the Jewish merchant and shopkeeper as difficult as possible. The Jews were forced to unionize to overcome, by joint efforts, the difficulties created by the government. The union's duties included providing credit to needy shopkeepers, explaining the endless new rules and regulations and affording legal support against all the controllers and inspectors who seized the opportunities to impose heavy monetary fines for 'breaches' of laws of commerce.

The union was formed by a few shopkeepers headed by Mr. Zeev Schneider who also served as its first chairman until his immigration to Israel in 1924 (He now lives in Rishon Le-Zion). He was succeeded by Dov Kyuchevsky, Yosef Vydenberg and others. The union's secretary and its " life and soul," till its last day was Binyamin Chorny.

The merchants thus set an example of a unified effort to overcome mutual difficulties. They were followed by artisans who finally attempted to create an organization too.

[Page 41]

The Artisans Union
(Craftsmen's Association)

In contrast to other small towns, A was also a town of Jewish craft and industry. Jewish artisans were inhabitants of the town from its earliest times. We can find an indication of the large artisan population in the many minyan's of observant craftsmen: the tailors' minyan, the shoemakers' minyan, and the mixed minyan where members were chiefly artisans: carpenters, blacksmiths, potters and others.

In these minyans, the members of worshippers reached the hundreds. We have no exact numbers of previous eras, but we do know that at the beginning of the century, the artisans (laborers formed about a third of the total Jewish population in Eishishok. and they constantly increased. It was due to this that also the Jewish Socialist Movement, the Bund, had a very strong hold in A. In 1905, the Bund had over 100 members in Eishishok. These were mainly young people, since the older people were usually employers and as such not acceptable by the Bund, even if they wanted to be. Artisans (such as tailors, watchmakers, and other " clean" craftsmen) were members also in other Socialist movements, such as Poalei Zion and later the S.S.

After several abortive attempts, craftsmen with a heightened sense of awareness and social consciousness, did succeed in 1924 to form an "Artisans Union." This organization embraced most of the town's artisans and assisted them considerably.

The heavy hand of the government was the main factor also in the formation of this union. The antisemitic Polish government attempted to pressure Jewish artisans out of business by burdening their lives. When the government realized that heavy taxes and arbitrary regulations would not scare the Jewish artisans, it invented a law requiring artisans to have a license.

Under the disguise of "concern for artisans' expertise," the government decided to force each artisan to undergo examinations testing his technical ability and knowledge of his trade and additionally, his knowledge of Polish.

Jewish artisans who were "old-hands" at their trades, were forced to prove to antisemitic officials that they indeed had mastered their craft. This created a wide opening to bribery, blackmail and persecution of the artisans by their examiners. The greatest torment was to prove knowledge, in reading and writing, of Polish, the language of the state, which most of the elderly artisans could not do. The artisans' union intervened on behalf of its members to ease the harsh decree enforced by the evil and ignorant examiner, and in many cases saved the livelihood of members who had failed the examination by proving that indeed they were experts and well deserved the license.

The union embraced approximately 180 families and its organizers were; Yehuda Leib Solomyanski, the watchmaker; Eltzik the barber; Koremin the tailor and others. The fact that they succeeded in organizing and preparing for public life a collection of people who were difficult to organize, helped promote the public image of the artisan and proved to be a great blessing.

[Page 42]

Some Figures Concerning Trade and Commerce in Eishishok

In the last years before World War II, the economic crisis began to have its effect and the shopkeepers and artisans were its victims.

Commerce depended on the farmers of the vicinity who sold their produce and purchased their needs on Thursday the market day or during the four yearly fairs.

During the thirties however, the number of Christian shops increased and these competed very successfully with the Jewish shops, since the former paid much lower taxes. Additionally, the chain of co-operative agricultural shops supported by the government widened, and the widened, and the farmer no longer depended on the Jewish shopkeepers. Thus many Jewish families lost their livelihood.

According to the statistics of 1936, 792 people in Eishishok made their living from commerce and shopkeeping. This includes some shops whose capital did not exceed a few dozen golden coins.

Jewish and Christian Shops

Type	1925		1935	
	Jews	Christians	Jews	Christians
Grocery	51	1	31	4
Fabric	22	-	11	-
Shoes and Fancy Goods	11	-	16	-
Restaurants & Pubs	13	-	15	5
Ready Made Clothes	4	-	7	-
Pharmacies	4	1	3	1
Leather	5	-	6	1
Iron	8	-	6	-
Miscellaneous	12	-	11	-
Total	130	2	106	11

These numbers show how the Christians slowly entered the market of Jewish livelihood and the number of their shops increased from 2 in 1925 to 11 in 1935 while the number of Jewish shops decreased in those 10 years. The competition was fierce and profits meagerly.

[Page 43]

Artisans
(23 Different Crafts)

332 families dealt in crafts. Of these there were 139 Jewish artisans and 55 apprentices; a total of 194. Of the Christians, there were 88 artisans and 50 apprentices: a total of 138. Of these there were 51 Jewish shoemakers and 57 Christians; 63 Jewish tailors and 19 Christians; 22 Jewish wheelmakers, cabinetmakers and carpenters and 8 Christians.

[Page 44]

The Professional Union of Workers

The number of laborers in Eishishok was relatively small. Most were members of the "Hachalutz-Haklali" and "Hamizpachi" organizations in the town. The minority whose beliefs resembled the Bund and Communists, organized themselves in a professional union of laborers with no division into the various professions. They were organized by Zeev Katz, an unbalanced individual who oscillated from one party to another with no compunction. Originally, he was an enthusiastic Zionist who actually immigrated to Israel but he quickly returned and became a Communist. He worked for the Polish secret police, was an enthusiastic Yiddishist and also knew Hebrew. With the force of rhetoric and energy, he succeeded to organize the handful of laborers in a "professional union" to fight the "battle of the classes" against the "bourgeois employers" i.e.; the tailors and the shoemakers, representatives of "private property" in the town, who in fact struggled to make ends meet and employed one or two laborers in their workshops.

This union provided a facade for the Communist Yiddishists who were an insignificant minority in the town. Their fight against Zionism was expressed in their resistance to the Zionist management of the general library. This library was the "bone of contention" and constant battle ground of the two camps: the Hebrews and the Yiddishists, Meetings for the election of the library management often ended in blows. Torn shirts and bloody noses were a frequent result of this language battle. The question of the amount of money to be assigned for the purchase of Hebrew books was a hard and painful problem, inciting "battles" which lasted for years. The weighty question of whether a Zionist or Yiddishist would be elected as chairman entailed a heavy war of schemes and strategies. And although the results were known from the outset, since most of the readers were members of the various Zionist organizations, this didn't decrease the fervor of the war. This was a war of beliefs, and in Eishishok, before its terrible destruction, the Jewish youths, so naive and enthusiastic, felt it was a matter of life and death!

[Page 47]

The Destruction of Eishishok

"Before the " Storm"

After the district of Vilna was "annexed" to Lithuania in 1939, Eishishok was only a few kilometers away from the Russian-Lithuanian border. It became a major passage for the many Jewish refugees who escaped from the Russian and German occupied Poland to the still independent state of Lithuania, which at that time, was a center of the Zionists-Hebrew movement and other Jewish movements, Vilna, the new capital of the enlarged Lithuania and referred to as the Jerusalem of Lithuania, was the main attraction since it still offered possibilities of immigration to Israel and other countries across the sea. And in this "between the wars" period, Eishishok had an important function as a "transit town" for thousands of refugees.

We now present the stories of three people who found temporary refuge in Eishishok along with thousands of others. They have nothing but admiration and praise for the Jews of Eishishok for their helping-hand, warm treatment, and the Jewish love which they offered their unhappy brothers.

In those difficult days, the Jews of Eishishok proved that they were indeed truly merciful. They provided the refugees not only with financial means to continue their journey to Vilna and Kovna, not only with "Kosher" documents, but also surrounded them with a warm and encouraging atmosphere which strengthened their hearts and gave some comfort to their sorrow.

The wonderful conduct of our townspeople is a living monument in the hearts of the thousands of refugees who met them and is a source of pride and appreciation for us the town's survivors.

[Page 48]

"Don't be afraid, we will get you out!"
Excerpt from the diary of a military translator 1939

M. Chodorovsky

Poland collapsed a few months ago. Its eastern part was "liberated" from freedom of speech, of movement, of press and even of food and clothing. Persecution of Zionists has begun.... there is an increasing desire to escape and many plans are laid to cross district, border, sea and continent to reach the country we have dreamed of from our youth on.

Only one way is open: through Vilna, Even there, chances are slim, but a prisoner will attempt to escape even through an invisible crack, The Belorussian-Lithuanian border is sealed tight, Lithuanian and Soviet authorities have tightened border security and chances of passing grow slimmer daily ... Yes, there is no choice, we must hurry or else it will be too late... We gathered in Lida, a couple of dozen kilometers away from the border. Our group consisted of 14 people. One woman with two children, an aged violinist with his handicapped son, three girls and the rest, young men of 20-25 years of age.

It was a cold night in the middle of 1940. When we stepped on the snow, it creaked and groaned, as if to inform on us. "Here goes a border smuggler." ... I will not forget that night as long as I live. Nine hours ... in straits, frozen puddles, a river, frost, ice, woods ... shots ... the weeping of the children and their mother, a frozen old man and his handicapped son, miserable, beside him ... the wailing of the girls and a cry of " Help!" Only nine of us reached the outskirts of Eishishok.

"Stop! Do you have any money?" demanded a tall Lithuanian policeman, the first to appear before me in the Lithuanian republic. Joseph Sh. began negotiating with him. We took off our watches and collected all of our valuables - we had no Lithuanian currency and he refused to accept Russian rubles.

Just as we finished with the first policeman, others appeared demanding more money. We told them we had no more valuables, since we had given all to the first policeman. We were promptly taken to the Eishishok. prison to sit there among the other " candidates" for Aliyah.

Through the prison windows, the faces of Eishishok. Jews peeped in. Many braved the cold to come greet us, give us breakfasts, encourage us and promise to help us.

"Do not fear, we will get you out"

During the day we were visited by the heads of the Jewish community of the town. They brought us food, linen and more encouraging words. The children of Eishishok. gathered round the prison asking us what else we needed. The elders issued orders, dispatched delegations, pledges were made, and finally we were freed.

Yes, our Eishishok stood the test and truly deserves its reputation as a "refuge for refugees." All 15,000 refugees who passed through the town praise it. It comforted, provided warmth, encouraged and gave provisions for the rest of the journey. And we do not mean only provisions of food but spiritual provisions as well and an increased will to survive and continue our wanderings to the shores of our homeland.

If you were lucky enough not to be spotted by a policeman, you could approach, in dark of the night, any Jewish home, without question, and be welcomed. They offered their beds and the beds of their children, rose to warm up tea, and helped you and your children.

Thus was the conduct of Eishishok. And therefore I dared, in a special song for Eishishok, to wish the Hebrew land of Israel, that it, too, will be blessed by such an Eishishok, on its Northern and Southern borders.

"Eishishok too, was destroyed, together with its dear and warm Jews," my fellow Joseph tells me with tears falling from his eyes.

Members of the Relief Committee in Eishishok

The Committee was founded in the early years after the First World War with the help andefficient support of the former residents of Eishishok in the United States of America. (sitting in the front row - Mr. Aharon Don (Becker), the emissary of the former residents of Eishishok in America)

[Page 50]

"The Warm-Hearted Jews..."
(by a Zionist " Border-Smuggler")
Published in " Haboker" (This Morning)

Shlomo Brener

After the Vilna district was given, by the Soviets, to the "independent" state of Lithuania, a widespread transfer of pioneers was organized from the Soviet part of Poland, where all Zionist activity was prohibited, to Vilna and Kovna. The Zionist movement, in all its different branches, flourished in Lithuania at that time, and the pioneer movement had many, many members.

When my native town, Lotzk, became part of Russia, I was forced, as a Zionist, to escape to Vilna. The " Hachalutz" center in Vilna assigned me the task of organizing the smuggling of pioneers from the Bialystok-Polsia district, across the Lithuanian-Russian border. I accepted the assignment and went to the town of Voronova, which served as a meeting place and last station before the border smuggling. Some Jews in the town had connections with reliable peasants who took pioneers and other Refugees over the border for 100-150 rubles a person. The money was given to the peasants, by the Voronova Jews, only after they presented a note signed by the head of the group indicating a safe arrival. This activity continued successfully for several months till the matter was brought to the attention of the Soviet authorities (mainly through the fault of our Communist brothers). The border security was consequently tightened and those caught were sentenced, administratively, to 15 years of exile in Siberia.

My name was brought to the attention of the Soviets as organizer of the smuggling activities, and they began to follow me. I had to act extremely cautiously. One day, sitting at the barber's in Voronova, I overheard one Jew, probably a Communist, telling his fellow that tonight they were going to bring an end to the Zionist gang.

I quickly shaved and left, pretending to have heard nothing. I hurried to the butcher, who served as a middle-man between the other involved Jews and me, and told him what I had heard. "Yes, I have heard of the matter." he told me, " The town is surrounded by policemen and N.K.V.D. detectives. This evening they intend to search for pioneers and refugees who are not natives of the town. You have to get out of here!"

"What shall I do?" I questioned him. " Where can I escape and hide? Give me some advice! You know what awaits us if I am caught by the police!"

The butcher thought for a moment and was suddenly struck with an idea. " Come, I have a place for you. I hope that even the Soviet eye won't be able to find you there."
He brought me to a storage house for wood, in the corner of which there was a two meter deep pit. He covered the pit with torn sacks, old clothes and boards, on top of which he placed dry wood. I lay hidden in that dark and airless hole for several hours. At midnight, I emerged and, assisted by one of our peasants, made my way across the fields to an isolated house in the woods where nine pioneers awaited me. I intended to make my last trip across the border with them to Eishishok, which served as the first station across the Lithuanian border. From Eishishok, the pioneers were sent to Vilna or Kovna to join pioneer training groups.

We walked in a single file, headed by the peasant. In the middle of our journey, in a big forest, the peasant disappeared, leaving us to ourselves. We didn't know the way nor where we were. We had to decide whether to return or continue alone and pray for a miracle to happen. We decided that no matter what happened, we would continue.

For us, Russia meant Siberia and hard labour camps in the Taigas. We walked for another two hours and came to a wooden pole lying across the way. We realized we had reached the border. The journey was arduous, the ground was frozen, and the walk across the forest paths (we dared not use the roads) was very difficult.

Each of us was also wearing several suits of clothes and underwear, the only property we could smuggle with us, and carrying backpacks. We had one girl with us. Suddenly as if springing from the earth, three peasants appeared. These were robbers who waited in ambush for refugees smuggling across the borders to rob them of their money. Frequently, they stripped their victims down to their underwear and sometimes even murdered them. They had pistols and demanded we accompany them to the Russian border station. We pled with them and gave them the rest of our money, but they were still not satisfied. They demanded gold and jewelry. One of us gave his watch, another, his only ring, the third gave clothing. They demanded more and more - and since we had no more to give them, they began beating us. We could not even shout for fear that the soldiers would hear us and we had no weapons. We were desperate. Finally, after pleading and begging them, they left us. Frightened and beaten, we mustered what was left of our strength and plodded on. We were exhausted and hungry and though frozen, we were covered with sweat from our encounter with death.

About an hour later we reached a small house faintly lit from within, standing on the outskirts of the village. We knocked and a peasant came to the door. We asked him to let us in to warm ourselves and he agreed. We found out later that he was one of the border smugglers and accustomed to such encounters. He informed us that we were on the village of Tavshun, about four kilometers away from Eishishok. For us, that meant that we were happily on Lithuanian territory. We sighed with relief and thanked G-d that we had safely crossed the border and escaped evil. The peasant knew the Jews in Eishishok who were involved in smuggling Jews across the border and agreed to escort us to them. We decided to leave the girl in the house with our belongings so that she could get some rest. The peasant's daughter, who appeared to be a quiet and honest Christian, remained with her. Thus, after a short rest, we started on our way to Eishishok. The peasant went ahead of us and we followed, scattered, about fifty meters behind him. About one kilometer away from his village, seven Lithuanian soldiers appeared. They beat the peasant and shouted at him. We did not understand the language. The peasant escaped and returned to his village. The soldiers surrounded us and thus we reached Eishishok at daybreak, on the first street we met Jews who looked at us with sympathy and compassion. One of them approached the soldier who appeared to be the officer of the group, and conferred with him for some minutes, hinting to us not to fear. We then went to a large house situated on the corner of two streets and belonging, as we later learned, to a warm-hearted Jew named Lubetzky.

We were received with a Jewish warmth that touched our hearts, given food and drink, and made to feel that we were among brothers. Upon a hint from the Jew, the soldiers left us. More Jews came to the house and we learned later that these were the members of the committee which took care of the refugees from Russia.

We told these warm-hearted Jews of the girl we had left behind in the village and they sent a coachman to bring her. We spent three days in Eishishok and liked the town immensely. Eishishok was full of refugees from all parts of Russia, Germany, and Poland. All found rest there after their hazardous journey. The " spirit" of the " Committee to Aid the Refugees" was the rabbi of the town, Rabbi Shimon Rozovsky, who had a majestic face and wise eyes and could also recite a good Jewish joke to hearten the spirits.

The members of the committee used to gather in his house. The work of the committee involved ransoming refugees caught by the Lithuanian authorities. It also obtained Lithuanian passes for the refugees so that after a few days rest, they could continue their journey to Vilna, the Lithuanian capital. Money was also provided by the committee for the first few days of the journey. All this was done with such Jewish warmth and heartiness that all who passed through the town in those turbulent days were full of praise for the pleasant town and its kind inhabitants.

On the fourth day the committee rented a truck to take 60 refugees to Vilna. This was necessary because the train did not pass through the town, and the buses, leaving from the marketplace station, were so full of people that strong elbows were necessary to get us on one. About one hundred kilometers away from the town, a Lithuanian police car, coming from the other direction, stopped the truck and began questioning as to who we were and what our destination was. We seemed suspicious and the driver was ordered to return us to the police station in the town. We knew that once the Lithuanian police discovered our identities, they would return us to the Russian border and we would be doomed to Siberia.

There was only one Lithuanian policeman with us and he was seated beside the driver. I and two other refugees, who on no account wished to face the Russians again, jumped off the truck when it reached the first street in Eishishok, Vilna Street, and disappeared among the houses. We returned to the house of the kind man who had accommodated us and told him what had happened. The committee was alerted and it decided to send another truck and transfer us to Vilna before the police would be able to conduct a wider investigation. Unfortunately, this truck was also stopped and we were all returned, under Lithuanian police guard, to the police chief. The police chief ordered the whole group, some 80 people, to be transported that same evening to the Russian border, which was located six kilometers from Eishishok. The night was dark and I decided to escape again, since returning to Russia was out of the question for me. We were escorted by 18 policemen. I slowly began to lag and fall behind the nearest policeman. When walking alongside of a ditch, I dropped to my belly, crawled to the ditch, and rolled into it. When the group had moved some distance from me, I began to run back to Eishishok. I heard the sounds of shouts and shooting behind me, but I safely reached the first house. I knocked on the window and a Jewish voice answered me. He took me in, I told him what had happened, and asked him to take me to the Lubetzky house where I had spent the previous night. Next morning, Mr. Lubetzky found me a place in a car going to Vilna…Two hours later I safely reached the "mother city of Israel", the "Jerusalem of Lithuania". I later learned that the whole group was returned safely to Eishishok. The dear Jews of that town had followed the policemen and on the order of their chief, whose heart was softened by a few hundred coins, returned them. I met many of that group in Vilna and together we reminisced about our mutual experiences in Eishishok and its wonderful people, whom I will never forget.

[Page 54]

Eishishok, Eishishok, how pleasant and beautiful you were
Excerpt from the book
" In the Storm on a Tempestuous Day"

Ben Zion Ben Shalom

We are going to Vilna. We arrive at a small town. At the station, an assistant of the man organizing the smuggling across the Russian-Lithuanian border awaits us. At midnight we leave the town. The skies are cloudy but the layer of snow affords some light. The pathless route is difficult. We cross fields and meadows " rich" with pits. The heavy back-pack is burdensome. One of the peasants heads the procession, the other brings up the rear. The Jew carrying the child is first on the line and I am last.

We have walked three hours already. Our guides promise us that in half an hour we shall reach the Lithuanian village across the border. We are at the end of our strength. We finally arrive at the first houses of the town. The town is asleep. Our guides knock on the door of one of the houses. We enter a small room lit by an oil lamp. My heart is full of happiness the like of which I have not experienced in years. My lips cannot move but all of me inside is whispering " Thank G-d I have lived to see this day!"

A heavenly morning. The earth is frozen but a wintry sun is shining. We walk the streets of the town and love every bit of it. Eishishok, Eishishok, how pleasant and beautiful you are! How every heart blesses you! We see your small, beautiful homes and your streets blessed with a special grace. You were so beautiful and perfect in our eyes that morning. Our first stop on Lithuanian soil! My pleasant town, we will remember you always with gratitude and love.

In that Jewish house we met the first group. Greetings were exchanged. They tell of their plights in passage and we tell of ours. In the corner the Jew's daughter is sitting doing her homework. I approach her. The books are Hebrew books and so is the lesson she is writing. Dear child, may you be blessed!

We spend that day in Eishishok. There is no train station here and it is very difficult to find room on the bus. We spent the night in the town. Next morning we "capture" places on the bus and after two hours drive, finally reach Vilna.

[Page 56]

The Holocaust

The Holocaust

Of 3,000 Eishishok Jews, most of whom were murdered by the defiled, only some few dozen survived. Some of the latter have already come to Israel. From the stories told us by those who were "snatched from the fire" we have compiled this chronicle of the destruction and terror which befell our beloved. The nightmarish scenes of the Jewish life in the town during the three months of the Nazi occupation till the day of slaughter, flash before our eyes. Eishishok was one of the few towns that the Nazis and their satellites vent their furor upon during the first months of occupation. Our pen has no strength to describe in full the horror and enormity of disaster which hit the Jews so suddenly. Only a fragment of the whole is described here, in the notes of the survivors who reached Israel.

The authors of these notes were eye-witnesses to all that happened to the Jews until their last day. They continued living lives of hidden "conversos" in the homes of " good Goys" who agreed, for huge sums of money, not to betray them to the Nazis and their Polish and Lithuanian collaborators. At a later period, once the Jews ran out of money, the "good Goy" cooperated no longer and they were forced to flee to the forests and join the partisans there. With them, they led a life of fear and danger but were at least encouraged by the feeling that they were fighting their enemy with arms and avenging the slaughtered.

The stories presented here are truthful; they are not exaggerated nor poetically adjusted. We read here the truth in all its horrible and horrifying simplicity.

[Page 57]
The Last Days of Eishishok

Shalom Ben Shemesh (Sonenson)

During the last years before the Russian and German occupation of Poland in 1939, the anti-Semitism greatly increased. Attacks on Jews walking through the streets of Eishishok became frequent. Drunken thugs, most of whom came from out-of-town, dared stand by the Jewish shops and forcefully prevent the entrance of Christian shoppers. On market-days the thugs, including some who wore uniforms of Polish students, assaulted the Jews, injured them physically and damaged their property. A venomous propaganda was launched against the "blood- suckers of the Polish people" and there were cries of "Jews go to Palestine!","Wait, cursed Jews, your fate will be like that of your German brothers, we will kill you without Hitler!" The Jews dreaded the Market Day on Thursday. If the day ended with some tavern windows smashed and only a few beatings, the Jews would thank the Heavens for their mercy. The atmosphere became more and more tense. Then the town's own Goys, who previously had few gleeful spectators, began showing signs that they too were willing to participate in the "holy" war against the Jewish "reign" in the town.

Thus the Polish people and leaders were too busy fighting the war against the "internal enemy" to have the will or time to anticipate the real danger from the west, where the enemy was insolently and openly preparing its arms and enjoying the confusion which overcame the Poles.

So when the Nazis invaded Poland on Sept 1, 1939 and captured more than half of the big country in a matter of days, it came as a dreadful surprise for both Poles and Jews. The danger of war had been much discussed but neither the leaders nor the people really believed that Hitler would dare carry out his threats.

The notorious Polish arrogance and the exaggerated faith in the strength and courage of the "splendid" Polish army and its great commander, the Marshal Ridz-Smigli (whom Pilsudsky himself had named as his successor and deputy) - blinded the Poles from seeing their economic and military weakness of Poland, divided and wasted by party fights and peoples' quarrels.

The rapid conquest of Poland and the disintegration of its army stupefied the Jews too. They had hoped that the army would prevent the advancement of the Nazis and hold out till the allies came to the rescue. With the approach of the Germans, the Jewish population was stricken with mortal fear. Their hearts dreaded the worst - and were not mistaken.

Treachery appeared from all sides. The " folksdentsdien", the Ukrainians, the White Russians and the Lithuanians - all gleefully watched the defeat of hated Poland and the bitter end anticipated for the Jews.

The Goys of Eishishok showed their hatred of the Jews and their pleasure at the fate awaiting them, though no one could have foreseen the immensity of the holocaust about to hit millions of Jews so rapidly.

On the 17th of September, 1939 troops of tanks and armored cars of the Red Army entered the town. Initially, rumors spread that the Russians had come to save and assist their Slavic Polish, brothers against the common enemy - the Teutonic beast. But all illusions and hopes quickly proved groundless - the bitter and bare reality was soon exposed.

A Revolutionary council ("Revkum") was founded in the town and headed by the communist Haim Shuster, a native of Eishishok. Its first decision was to prohibit the various Zionist organizations in the town and transform the Hebrew reactionary school to a proletarian Yiddish school. The Eishishok Bourgeoisie children were expelled in shame from their school which was intended only for children of the " working" and " oppressed" classes.

But the Communist rule did not last long. A month later, the district of Vilna including Eishishok, became part of the "friendly" state of Lithuania and the Lithuanian rule substituted the Russian. This year, 1939-1940, was the year of light preceding the darkness.

The Communists and their families left the town together with the Red Army which remained in the big cities only. The Zionist groups renewed their activities and the school became Hebrew again. The Jews adjusted quickly to the new government and business flourished. Connections with the Lithuanian Jews were renewed after a forced severance of over 20 years.

Eishishok, situated close to the Lithuanian White Russian border, served as a transit station for thousands of refugees who escaped from Russian and German occupied Poland. The refugees smuggled over the border at time in mortal danger. But when they arrived at Eishishok, they found there a brotherly hand ready to help them. Eishishok's committee to aid the refugees was organized, headed by the community's Rabbi, Rabbi Shimon Rozovsky, may he rest in peace. This committee provided the refugees with money and " kosher" documents and sent them to the capitol, Vilna.
The Rabbi's house was full of devoted community workers and the town's streets were full of authors and biblical scholars. But this era of splendour did not last. In June of 1940, Lithuanians entered the Russian Soviet pact and the reign of the local Communist Jews, in all its terror, returned. This time they were harder. Arrests and persecution began. Zionism was prohibited, Hebrew was declared a " reactionary" language and the shops of the " big bourgeoisie" were confiscated and their owners had to find other employment. Among the confiscated shops were Abeliov's, Kyuchevsky's, Koppelman's, Veidenberg's and others, (Abliov became a blacksmith, Markel Koppelman - a clerk in a Vilna pharmacy, etc.). Merchandise was scarce and prices soared, searches and fines became daily incidents. But most of the Jews seemed somehow to manage also under Soviet rule. The Black Market flourished.

A Communist party was established in the town, headed by Libke Ginunsky, an Eishishok girl, who served a five year prison term under the Poles on account of her Communist beliefs. The "Komsomol" was headed by the Communist Reuvaleh, son of Shmuel the Shoemaker (nicknamed Di "Bolvitzke").

Life became increasingly more difficult but the Jews comforted themselves with the fact that Jew-haters were forced to conceal their feelings and mainly because they had been spared Hitler - the undiscriminating Jew hater.

And then the Russian-German war broke out. Already on the second day of the war, the 23rd of June, 1941, Nazi troops entered the village. The Russians retreated, offering no resistance. The Vilna-Bialystok Road crossed Eishishok, and the German invaders' march through the town lasted two weeks. There was a steady stream of tanks, cars, cannons, and military personnel of all kinds which continued day and night. The immense force proceeded in three columns, heading east. The window panes trembled from the sounds of the heavy wheels. The Jews dared not emerge from their homes. Seized with deathly fear they sat behind their closed blinds and doors listening to the echoes of the triumphant Nazi march and the joyous shouts of the Goys lining the road sides and hailing their "saviours" from the "Judo-Communist" rule.

When the huge stream decreased and only the German troop remained to guard the town, the Jews emerged to the streets, with faces pale and eyes expressing despair and fear of the future.

The German army had not yet harmed the Jews. They only declared contemptuously " The Jews will go away from here", and the Jews did not yet comprehend the meaning of the sentence. A division of the Ministry for Public Works, which was founded by Todt, came to the town. Eishishok's decree was issued ordering all men 16 to 60 years old to report and register for work. Any evader who would be caught-would be shot. The work involved repairing the road. Leading from Eishishok to Vilna. Each work day lasted 14 hours, from 7 a.m. to 9 p.m. One half hour break was allowed for lunch. The pay was 50 pfennigs. Since the work site was 10 km away from Eishishok and one had to report there before 7 a.m., the men set out at 5 a.m. and returned at 11 p.m. The guards were " folksdeutsche" that is Polish citizens of German origin, who had settled in Poland hundreds of years before but once the Germans took over, they betrayed Poland and resumed their " German" identity. These people were horrible sadists who surpassed the Germans in their cruelty. They tortured us in various ways. After an exhausting day's work, when we were hungry and tired to the bone, we were forced to perform military exercises- to strip naked and beat each other to the defiled merriment of our guards … the officer Weber surpassed the others in cruelty.

Two weeks later a new military commander came to town. He summoned Rabbi Rozovsky, may he rest in peace, to his headquarters (the Kyuchevsky house) and ordered us to organize a 12 member Jewish committee (Juden Comitat).

"You cursed Jews are responsible for all wars, and therefore you must pay a high price-and you certainly will" He ended his barking order and ordered the Rabbi to leave his presence immediately. Rabbi Rozovsky gathered the men in the synagogue and informed them of the order. There were no eager volunteers for this duty. It was decided to choose the members by lot. The names which came up were Avraham Kaplan - who served as chairman, S. Sonenson-deputy chairman, Yehuda Dvilansky, watchmaker Zelig Sevitzky, Itzi Mendel Yurkansky, Yosef Michalovsky, Ephraim Karnovsky,(son in law of Bara Yankil Reznik, the last chairman of the Eishishok community before the war) Hanan Michlovsky, Mordechai Kaganovitz, Markel Koppelman and others.

Some days passed and a troop of border guards came to the town instead of a military troop. Torture began. The committee was ordered to prepare big boxes and inform the Jews to bring all their jewelry and silver and gold coins to headquarters. This booty was put in the boxes and sent to the " fatherland" - Germany. New orders were issued daily. They demanded cigarettes, wine, cakes, eggs, butter. All orders had to be supplied by the committee within a few hours or days. Delays were paid for by murderous beatings. The Lithuanian police eventually also came to town, headed by the murderer Ostrovaskas and the committee was thenceforth obliged to fulfill the greedy demands of both Germans and Lithuanians.

The German border-guards maltreated us with various tortures; their sick and sadistic minds invented new methods daily. They frequently robbed us, the committee members, downstairs, set their dogs on us, rushed us to headquarters several times daily for trivialities and fired their guns above our heads for amusement.

On the Saturday, Rosh Hodesh of Elul, the Germans and their Lithuanian assistants, seized a group of men, led them to the river near the bridge on Vilna Street, forced them to bathe, fully clothed, in the river and then to roll on the road in order to clean it of dust. Finally they set their dogs on them and drove them home.

One day they gathered 250 bearded Jews in the market place. They arranged them in two rows and ordered them to pluck out each other's' beards. The wretched victims were surrounded by the defiled sadists who made sure no one was cheating. The whips whistled and mercilessly lashed at heads and bodies. The scene was accompanied by the wild laughter of the murderers and village Goys who had gathered to watch the amusing spectacle

One day when Mordechai Kaganovitz and myself had come to headquarters we were ordered to strip to our waists and climb up to the roof. Fire engines of the fire department were brought and my brother Moshe was ordered to direct torrents of water upon us to throw us off the roof. We held on to the tiles and chimney with all our strength. Our arms froze and our fingers became paralyzed from the cold and effort but we managed to hold on. After half an hour of wild laughter of the Germans and Goys we were allowed to descend and we fled home.

Before leaving the town, they robbed us of everything. They stripped the schools of decorations and took the ancient candlesticks. They broke the benches of the synagogue and burnt the books of the public library in the market place.

They desecrated the cemetery by breaking the gravestones. They destroyed the bath house and the Mikveh. The Teutonic vandals showed their face. Eventually, the rule over the town was transferred to the Lithuanian police and the latter expressly showed that they surpassed the Nazis in cruelty and hatred for Jews.

Peasants began to spread rumours that towns were emptying of their Jews and that the Jews were being murdered en masse. These peasants suggested the Jews turn their goods over to them rather than let the Lithuanians enjoy the spoils. " Your end will come anyway" they said in feigned sympathy. But we did not want to believe these terrible rumours. We deluded our-selves that we, perhaps, would be saved. The catastrophe would not reach us, we hoped. Our will to survive was very strong. We believed the oppressors would take all our belongings, starve us and torture us, that the weak would not withstand the torture but that the strong would survive. We held with all our strength to the board of life floating precariously on the waves of hatred and suffering. Only a small number realized the truth and said " We are all lost". No one will survive this hell. One of these was Rebbe Shimon Rozovsky, may he rest in peace. When he was informed that many Jews hid money, jewelry and valuables with their Christian acquaintances, he called the community leaders and warned them not to hand over any more of the remaining goods to the Goys.

"You will cause the Goys to be your deadly enemies if you hand over the rest of your goods. They'll be the first who will want to get rid of your to enjoy the spoils", reiterated the wise Rabbi but no one heeded.

Each of us hoped in his heart that he would be saved and therefore wished to protect what remained of this belongings for his life after the war. And the boiled chilling rumors of the extermination of Jews of the adjacent villages persisted. When we learned of the slaughtering of the Jews of the town of Aran we sent a reliable Goy to check out the rumour. The latter returned and told us that the streets of Aran were still full of unburied Jewish bodies rolling in the dust. Yet many of us still refused to face the appalling reality and tried to continue the life of illusion and unfounded hopes.

The Rabbi again gathered the community leaders and told them: " Jews, you see our end is approaching rapidly... G-d did not want us to be saved. Our destiny has been decided, and we must accept this. But if we must die – let us at least die honorably. We must not hold out our necks like sheep brought to slaughter. With the money we still have, let us buy weapons and protect ourselves till our last breath. Anyway our money is worthless. We must not go to slaughter like a flock of sheep! Let us die but take the Philistines along!"

Ephraim Karnovsky supported the rabbi but Yosel Veidenberg attacked him in fury: " You want war? Your want to bring destruction on our whole community and on all the Jews" Each day a miracle might still happen and we will be saved-we must not give up hope.. What is our strength when compared to the enemy's? You don't care", we told Ephraim Karnovsky " you are a stranger here-but I tell you, they want only to plunder our money and possessions-they will not butcher us all!"

Opinions were divided and the meeting ended with no decision taken and no preparation made. Meanwhile the Lithuanian commander, the murderer Ostrovakas announced that if we would give him 1000 rubles in gold he would protect us from the destruction awaiting us.

This roused more hopes and illusions. No gold or silver coins remained but gold rings and jewelry were quickly collected and demanded as " ransom" to the murderer. Hope and fear mingled in our hearts.

On Sunday, Rosh Hashana eve of 5702 (1941) Wolf, the district commander in Vilna, issued an urgent order that the Jews hand over to the police, during that day, all their money and good clothing.

The order stated that if money or valuable clothes would be found in any house, all the family members would be murdered. The committee realized that the, end had come.

And indeed, the day of judgment had arrived. We, the committee members, went from house to house that evening advising everyone to escape. But where? We ourselves did not know-each person must find some hiding place and escape as best he could. The main thing was to escape for time was running out. That same day the Jews of the towns of Olkeniki and Selo - about 1000 people in all -were brought to Eishishok and put in the stables near the " Gemina" in the village of Yurzdiki.

They were told that they were on their way to Eishishok where they would live in a ghetto. Next morning, the first day of Rosh Hashanna, all the Jews of the town including their children and babies were ordered to gather in the two schools and synagogue. Any person found in his house would be shot on the spot.

Many Lithuanian policemen - another big troop of Lithuanian and German soldiers had recently arrived - went through the houses to check whether any Jews remained. I decided not to go to the school. My house stood at the edge of the village and I decided to escape. All that day the members of my household and myself hid in the stable amidst boards and sacks. We heard the murderous shouts of the policemen and the cries of beaten children. At eight o'clock that night my wife, my two children and myself escaped through the fields till we reached the " Sanidvor" forest. There we found Shlomo Kyuchevsky, his brother in law Yefim Shifel, Reuven Kaleko and his brother in law Leib Kovensky with this wife, children and elderly father, Aita Shishka, (84 years old). We decided to divide into two groups, one of which would head for Voronova and the other for Radun. Both towns belonged to Belorussia. had no ghettos and in both the Jews still had some freedom of movement. My family and myself reached Radun. We later learned that 490 people had escaped from

Eishishok on that day. Most were killed by Germans, Lithuanians and native peasants. Bluma Michalovsky and her sister were shot on the Lithuanian-Russian border, not far from Radun.

They were given a Jewish burial in Radun - the lucky ones! The graves of the rest are unknown. We sent a Goy from Radun to Eishishok to find out what was happening there. Only some days later we learned details of the dreadful tragedy from the Jew who succeeded to escape.

During the two days of Rosh Hashanah, 4000 Jews, men, women and children, were locked in the two schools and synagogue with no food or water. They also had to relieve themselves inside. On the third day of Tishre they were taken out of the buildings, arranged in four rows and led to the animal market on Radun Street.

The rabbi and the cantor led the procession. The cantor loudly recited the Vidui (the confessional prayer before death) and the whole community, weeping and crying, echoed the prayer. The death procession included the Olkeniki Jews who had been brought from Yurzdiki. There was no escaping. The market place was surrounded by German and Lithuanian troops. The crowd of Jews stood there all night. Daybreak dawned on the fourth day of Tishre, 5702, the last day in the lives of those thousands of people. From afar, the Jews saw Goys walking in the direction of the old cemetery with spades in their hands.

At 8 a.m. that morning, the Lithuanian police commander Ostrovakas chose 250 of the youngest and healthiest men and took them in an unknown direction. Each hour they took another group of men. To calm the agitated crowd, the Lithuanian hangman brought a forged letter from Leib Minkovsky, written in Polish. It read, "We are in Seklotzky yard preparing a ghetto for you. Do not fear. My wife, and I are waiting for you."

This letter raised hope again in many hearts so no objection was made when 250 additional men were taken. At 4 p.m. no men remained in the crowd, all had been butchered by the wild beasts in the old cemetery. Next morning, the Thursday, the same was repeated with the women and children.

The butcher Ostrovakas dressed in a white apron and wearing gloves was constantly on the scene in the old cemetery. With his own hands he shot children and threw them, while still alive and quivering, to the pits prepared by the native Goys. This was told to us by a Goy who was witness. But the rabbi's torture was not over yet. He had to drink his cup of agony to the last dregs. On the order of the sadistic butcher Ostrovakas, the rabbi was to be present in the cemetery all the while to witness the destruction of his community. Only at the end did the murderer have pity and shoot him and thus deliver the last Rabbi of Eishishok from this defiled and miserable world.

HaRav HaGaon, Naftali Menachem (Hertz-Mendel) Hutner, son of the rabbi, R' Yosef Zundel, who was a judge and a rabbi in Eishishok after the death of his father - he was also the last judge in Eishishok - gentle and noble - modest and virtuous

According to the testimony of survivors from Eishishok, who arrived to Israel, only these two tombstones, that the defiled hand of the Nazis didn't touch, remained in the new cemetery in Eishishok. They're the tombstones of thousands of martyrs from Eishishok who weren't brought to a Jewish grave.

[Page 67]

In Hiding

Yaffa, daughter of Moshe Sonenson (10 years old)

…when the Lithuanian policemen broke into the Jewish houses to hurry the Jews to the School buildings, my brother Itzhak and I hid in the storage hut for wood in our yard where we lay all day. We heard the scoldings and curse of the policemen, the shouts of beaten Jews and the cries of children. My father had escaped the day before but my mother with my one year old brother could not escape. She also didn't manage to reach the storage hut where we were hiding and so was taken to the synagogue. Before leaving my father told us that if we managed to avoid the policemen we should escape to a Goy who was a good acquaintance of ours, who would hide us. When evening came, and the village was quiet we left the hut and made our way through the fields and gardens to the house of Yashka Elyashkovitz who was a worker in our tannery.

His house was located at the edge of the village. He received us kindly and dressed my brother in the clothes of a Christian boy. There we found the children of David Moshtzenik, the girl Mira, her younger brother Meir and some other Jews. Yashka calmed us and we fell asleep from tiredness and fear.

Towards morning the Goy woke us and transferred us to the house of another Christian, located at the end of Pigs' street. I began to cry and demanded to be taken to my mother. All explanations and pleadings were to no avail. The Goy agreed to take me to the synagogue. On the way we met a Lithuanian policeman who told us that Christians were forbidden to walk the streets at that time. We had to return to the worker's house where I spent the whole day crying.

In the afternoon a young Christian came and told us he had been sent by my father to take us to him to the village " Dumbliyeh". That night the Christian put me on his shoulders and took me and my brother, who was dressed in the attire of a Christian shepherd, to Dumbliyeh. There we found father and the family of Sarah Kabatznik. For five days we hid in a barn belonging to a peasant lady who was an acquaintance of ours. At night she brought us food. During the day we dared not expose ourselves. On the sixth day, the Christian lady told us that she was too scared to hide us any longer for fear we would be discovered on her ground. She transferred us to her brother's house in the village Poradun.. At his house we saw many stolen Jewish articles brought from Eishishok, among them our own brass menorah. The peasant told us that all Eishishok Jews had been killed.

We did not trust him and we decided to leave his house. At night my father, brother and myself made our way through fields and woods to the village Vasilishok, considered part of Poland, unlike Eishishok which was considered Lithuanian. We found refuge in the house of a Polish acquaintance. But he demanded that my father go register with the police - or else he would be too afraid to keep us in his house. The police chief there was a Pole by the name of Smigola, a real Jew oppressor who ordered my father to jail for coming with no license from Lithuania.

Once Smigola spotted me bringing my father a bottle of milk. He became very angry and smashed the bottle. He drove me away with curses and threats. Only 10 days after being jailed was my father freed due to Jewish efforts and a large ransom.

Meanwhile we learned that mother and the baby had safely reached Radun. My mother disguised herself as a Christian and with the help of a Christian acquaintance, who said my mother was her sister, was allowed by drunken Lithuanian police to cross the border. But shortly after that, one of the policemen began to suspect and chase her. When my mother apprehended the danger, she threw the baby beneath a hay pile and herself hid in a second one. When the policeman saw no one he returned to the town. My mother emerged, took the baby who luckily had not cried, and reached Radun.

We arrived at Radun where a ghetto had been established, and there found my mother and brother. One day the Germans spread the rumor that the Russians were coming and pretended to pack their belongings and prepare themselves for flight. A few moments later, we heard sounds of shrieks and shooting. The Germans surrounded the ghetto, gathered the Jews in the marketplace, selected the young and healthy, and shot the rest on the spot.

We hid with 16 other Jews in an attic waiting for the end. Suddenly the baby began crying and we were struck with deathly fear. Surely the Germans would hear the baby and discover our hiding place! The Jews began whispering among themselves while mother tried to breast-feed the baby but the poor thing would not calm down and only cried louder. The whispering increased and one Jew said - we must " silence" the baby; 16 adult lives were more valuable than the life of one baby. Mother was paralyzed and froze and did not answer. The Jew took an article of clothing and threw it on the crying baby. Its cries ceased...we sat there frozen. Mother fainted.

Next day the remaining Jews were gathered together with those caught by the murderers. Anyone over 50 was shot. The rest had to bury them in a mass grave and cover the bodies with limestone.

After that things quieted down a bit. The searches and killings stopped. We descended from the attic and lived with the survivors in the Ghetto. On the day the surviving Radun Jews were transferred to the Lida ghetto, we managed to escape with some other Jews to the village Kurkushani where a Goy acquaintance of ours hid us for a large sum of money. This peasant dug a big pit in a pig pen, covered it with boards and on the boards heaped sacks and potatoes. We lived in that pit for a whole year, my father, mother, brother Itzhak, a girl from Olita and myself.

When we ran out of money, my father, disguised as a peasant ,went with the Goy to Eishishok took money from a hiding place on our house and gave it to the Goy. After that, the Goy became more and more impudent. He demanded more money for the potatoes he fed us daily and threatened to betray us to the Germans if we did not hand over all our money.

The pit was horribly smelly and suffocating. Our diet consisted nearly solely of potatoes and turnips.. and when we ran out of money the Goy made us leave. At night we returned to the village Lebetznik where we found Uncle Shalom and his daughter Gitele. We lived there for another year in a pit which we dug in a storage house of a peasant acquaintance whom we paid well. And once again we were forced to leave our hideout and escape to the forests. We joined the partisans who began appearing at that time. We lived there in danger and suffering till the Russians came and we returned to Eishishok. In an attack by Polish partisans, my mother and her baby were killed. My father was arrested and sentenced to eight years imprisonment due to a false charge of the Goys. I reached Israel with my Uncle Shalom who became an Israeli citizen.

I hope to see my father again and my brother Itzhak who remained in Russia - here in our country.

[Page 70]

With the Partisans

Rachel Potchter

When the Germans came to Eishishok all economic and public life came to a halt. Shops were closed and houses bolted. Initially no one dared leave his house. Everyone sat behind the locked doors and blinds with the fear of death in their eyes. When steps were heard approaching the house, the heart stopped beating.

During the first weeks a ceaseless stream of Hitler's soldiers passed through the town day and night. Tanks and cars of all kinds streamed through like a wide river. Even when the stream of soldiers ended and the town quieted down, people dared not emerge though walking outside was permitted till 6 p.m. Jews, of course, were not allowed on the sidewalks, only in the channels alongside them and had to wear the " yellow patch" on the tack and chest. But who felt like walking outside meeting a German or a Lithuanian policeman and being abused? People went outside as seldom as possible and then only when absolutely necessary to bring water from the nearby well or to go on the forced labor of the Germans.

Peasants from the vicinity no longer came to town to buy or sell their produce. Anyone caught buying from or selling to a Jew was punished. But food was not a serious problem since every house had supplies of flour, sugar, potatoes etc. prepared back in the days of Russian occupation. The poor were provided for by neighbors or the Jewish Council. Jewish neighborliness and brotherhood in need were revealed in all their beauty. But the terrible unknown future depressed the spirits and the evil tidings carried by peasant acquaintances, which stole their way into Jewish homes, made hair stand on end with fear and desperation. The synagogue and schools were closed even on Shabbat. People dared not congregate to draw comfort and strength from each other. The terror of the German and his cruel collaborator, the Lithuanian policeman, had struck us all. On the fourth day we were taken out of the school in rows and led together-men women and children, to the new horses market on Radun St. Till the last moment many deluded themselves that the Lithuanians and Germans were setting up a ghetto. It was inconceivable that we were actually being led to slaughter...

When the Lithuanian commandant arrived, Yosel Vydenberg approached him and asked what he planned to do with the Jews? In response, the commandant ordered him to head the group of healthy men who were later led in an unknown direction. We thought they were being led to work. We did indeed hear gun shots from afar but thought they were only intended to frighten. We did not yet realize the horrible truth. The Goys who went to see what was being done with the Jews came back and told us they were being led to the old cemetery and shot there. But we did not even believe them....And each two hours the policemen came and took another group of men...

Towards evening only the women and children remained. Evening came. Hundreds of women and children lay down on the ground in the horse market yard in a state of hunger and total exhaustion. The horrible naked truth was exposed. We had no strength even for tears. We lay there stunned and paralyzed awaiting daybreak. In the middle of the night a peasant who was a good acquaintance of mine, stole through the boards of the fence which surrounded the market and told me, Aitka Kaniuchovsky and Shoshanna Yurkanesky: " If you want to live - escape immediately before the light of day". We decided to escape. My two sons and myself (my husband had been killed that day) along with Aitka and her two sons, Shoshanna arid her son and another girl moved a board in the fence, escaped through the opening and were on our way: The police guards were far away from us.

The good peasant led us to the village of Dutzishok to the house of another peasant who was also a good acquaintance of ours. He fed us and we sent him to Eishishok to find out what was happening there. He returned and told us that there were no more Jews in the village. I decided to go to Benyakoni since the peasant was afraid to keep us in his house. There I found my two sons.

Later Haikel Kanichovsky, his wife Gutta and their two sons joined us. When the Germans ordered all Jews in the vicinity to assemble at Voronova, to the ghetto about to be set up, I decided not to go. My heart told me that a ghetto spelled certain death. Despite my family's objections I decided to disguise myself as a peasant, return to the Eishishok vicinity and find refuge at one of our peasant acquaintances with whom we had ties of friendship and business for years....and so I did. Dressed as a Goy and barefooted I went on my way. I reached the Eishishok vicinity and in a field there, I met a Goy who was a good acquaintance of ours. I told him of my intention. He too advised me against entering the ghetto - he told me to fetch my sons while he would think of some plan and place to hide us.

I returned to Benyakoni and succeeded in transferring my children disguised as peasants. This peasant was a " sultis" and on authority of his servant, the Germans and Lithuanians came and went freely in his house. His house therefore was not a possible refuge for us. A Jew, days later, came and told us that the " Bagmina" (the village committee) suspected him of hiding Jews. He was very sorry but he could accommodate us no longer, his life was in danger! According to the " law" a peasant caught hiding Jews was sentenced to death.

It was the beginning of November. The earth was already frozen and snow had already begun falling...Where should we go? I remembered that we had some acquaintances in the village of Yurtzishky. I begged the peasant to lead us to this village and point out to us, from a distance, the house of my peasant friend. This would spare me the search for the house and the danger such a search could entail of falling in the hands of policemen or anti-Semitic Goys. He agreed. On Sabbath morning we left and made our way through forests and fields until we reached the outskirts of the village. From there the peasant pointed out the house we were looking for. I knocked on the door and the peasant came out. When he saw me he shouted in amazement: " Good G-d! They told me you too were killed!" He took us in his house, fed us and hid us in his pantry for a few days . But since his house stood on the road he suggested transferring us to his sister who lived in an isolated house in a big forest far from the highway.

We accepted his generous suggestion gladly and gratefully. At night we set out for his sister's house, located about two kilometers away from the village, hidden in the thick of the forest and hence not at all visible from a distance. Her house was clean, beautiful and new and our hearts were gladdened. She welcomed us warmly. She was a wise and good hearted woman but poor. The monetary question did not disturb me. Before the war we had hidden a large amount of merchandise from our store in the homes of many peasants. Many debts owed to us were also outstanding.

In exchange for the merchandise, paid for by honest peasants, I was able to obtain enough food and also pay the peasant woman for our food expenses. To my request that we be allowed to spend at least two weeks in her house, the woman responded: " You can stay as long as you like, the war will not end so soon..."

We stayed for six months at her house. During the day we all remained in one room, and hardly emerged. Nevertheless inhabitants of the adjacent village began whispering that the woman was hiding Jews and we felt we must continue our wanderings in search for a new hideout. We decided to dig a pit in the forest and hide there.

In June of 1942, my sons and I dug a pit 1.20 meters deep and 2 meters wide and set up a stove of stones. We lived in that pit for eight months. When it rained the pit filled with water and we had to dig another pit somewhere else in the forest. In the second pit we lived for seven months. We obtained food through the peasant woman who did not know the location of our second pit. It was I who always approached her. We knew the truth of the proverb " Happy is the man who is constantly afraid". We uprooted a hollow tree, erected it on the entrance to our pit and entered the pit by sliding down the hollow.

In the forest I met a Soviet soldier who was also in hiding. He helped us a great deal in finding food which had become hard to obtain. White Polish partisans appeared in the forest. These fought not only the Germans but also and mainly against the Red Partisans. Their hatred of the Jews was boundless and any Jewish partisan or refugee who fell in their hands was killed on the spot.

We realized the situation was becoming unbearable. Food was hard to obtain and we could not approach the village since most of the peasants supported and assisted the White partisans. We therefore decided to try to reach the " Red" partisans, among whom, we heard, there were many Jews.

My elder son decided to try his luck at locating these partisans. After many attempts, he came upon a troop of Jewish and Russian partisans. When he told them of our plight their leader agreed to accept us.

One dark night, it was already the beginning of 1944, we took our few belongings and set out. We entered the " Podborze" forest. White partisans appeared in that forest and we were in great danger. To our luck we met a reconnaissance group of Russian partisans and told them who we were and of our wish to join them. They demanded weapons and would not let us enter the forest) without any. After much pleading and when we showed them the note the partisan leader had given my son they agreed to let us enter the forest. On the way we were stopped by hidden and well camouflaged partisan spotters.

"Do you have weapons? No? And money, do you have? Also not? In that case we cannot let you join the partisans". They agreed to accept my elder son but not my younger son or myself. We did not agree to these terms. We would neither move on nor return. We lay on the snow for six days. The partisans brought us food. One day a Jewish partisan girl came to us and told us in the name of the Partisan commandant to go to the " Visinche" forest. I told her there were White polish partisans in that forest.

"I refuse to go there! If he wants to kill me-let him kill me here. I don't care about anything!..." Finally I "won" and the three of us were accepted to the partisans. I was employed in the kitchen, my elder son in the reconnaissance troop and my youngest, in the spotters. So we were "useful" after all. To our luck, Russian planes brought weapons at that time, and in a quantity sufficient for every- one so the partisans resigned themselves to the fact that we had come weaponless and penniless.

We stayed with the partisans for four months till July of 1944. When the Russians liberated us we reached Vilna and from there we returned to Eishishok. We lived in Eishishok with the other survivors till the big attack of the Polish partisans. In that attack, Ziporah Sonenson and her child were killed. My elder son, driving in a car to Vilna to bring our belongings back to Eishishok was also wounded in his right leg by White partisans and after an illness which lasted nearly a year-he died in Lodz. My younger son and myself, left the valley of death, the Poland soaked with our blood, and after many plights, finally reached our homeland.

[Page 75]

From a Prison Camp to a Partisan Troop

Shneor Glembotzky

When the Polish-German war broke out I was stationed with my regiment in Vilna. I had been in service for a year at the time. My regiment and others were transferred by train west to Warsaw. But the frequent bombings by the "Luftwaffe" forced us to leave the train cars several times a day and hide in the woods and fields.

As we were traveling with no protection we were at the mercy of the German pilots. On the third of September we finally reached Siedlce but from the east, the direction we had come from, streamed the stunned and beaten Polish troops. The hasty and frightened retreat of the Polish army had begun. Its commanders had "lost their heads" already during the first days of war. Each regiment or rather each company, mindful of its own interest, followed its own plans and proceeded where it wished. Weapons of all kinds were scattered on roadsides. The German army which advanced into Poland from all directions, assisted by numerous fifth columnists, surrounded whole troops and took them into captivity. The situation was utterly chaotic. We threw away our guns, split into groups and each group attempted to find its way through the forests to its village. Not far from the city of Wyszkow our troop, consisting of approximately 200 men, was surrounded by the German army and taken prisoner. But on that day a big troop of Polish cavaliers appeared on the road and the Germans fled to the woods. We continued on our way and were taken captive again. We succeeded in escaping again. The fourth time we were taken captive by a mechanized troop and imprisoned in the prison camp at Siedlce, near Warsaw, where many thousands of Poles were held. We lay there on the ground for six days without food. The Germans paid us no attention and showed no interest in us. The badly wounded lay moaning and died. Officers and soldiers in torn, filthy clothes, hungry and lice infested, rolled on the cold ground cursing out loud.

Our hearts were struck with bitterness and despair. The terrible and shameful defeat combined with the hunger, cold and filth needed a scapegoat to provide an outlet for the anger and bitterness. The Jewish soldier served as a target for the fury. Anti-Semitism exposed its evil face. Phrases of brotherhood and friendship voiced at the outset of the war, when the Poles demanded all minorities to combine forces and save the common fatherland, were now forgotten.

Beatings of Jewish soldiers, curses, offenses and accusations that Jews had caused the war and Polish defeat increased constantly. The Germans did not intervene. On the seventh day of our arrival, we were loaded on freight cars and transported to Kenisberg and there divided into groups according to race: Polish, Ukrainian, Belorussian, and Jewish.

The guards of the camps were " folksdeutschen" - Polish citizens of German origin who declared their German identity and surpassed even the real Germans in their cruelty towards the Jews. Polish prisoners attacked the Jewish prisoners, a few hundred in number, seized their boots and clothes, leaving them in their underwear. The days were cold and the nights colder. The first snow had already begun falling. We were not spared beatings.

The food ration consisted of 200 grams of bread a day. Berke Kaganovitz and Yona Tavshunsky were in the same troop with me. Two weeks later we were loaded again on freight cars used for transportation of beasts and taken to a village called " Klein Deksin". From there to the prisoners camp we proceeded on foot. We passed a German farm on the way. A German boy was standing there beside the fence holding two apples. Berke Kaganovitz left the line, snatched the two apples and returned to the line. The boy began shouting and the guards began shooting but Berke mingled with the other soldiers and was not detected. Those two apples shared among us were our only food for two days. After two hours marching we reached the camp. A representative of the German sanitary committee was standing at the gate. We were ordered to undress in the cold; it was 25 degrees below zero. The medical orderly dipped a pen in ink and gave us injections against typhus! This was their preventive medicine against typhus! The next day we were dressed in clothes which were mere rags.

Our work consisted of cleaning the roads or constructing huts. We rose at 6 a.m., organized ourselves and then were divided into work groups under the supervision of armed Germans. We worked till 6 p.m. The food ration consisted of 200 grams of bread a day, occasionally a little margarine and at noon turnip soup containing no fat. The Jews were given the most difficult and vile jobs. The German citizens treated us brutally. Each step we took was accompanied by a stream of beatings, kickings and cursing. With sticks, rifle butts and kicks they beat us to amuse themselves and satisfy their sadistic instincts. In that prisoner camp we met the photographer Leibovitz, the son of the teacher Shaul Lidsky, Leizer Stutsinsky and Meir Shimon Politatsky.

One day several hundred prisoners were taken to clear the road of snow for a military procession. Yona Tavshunsky was beaten by a German policeman and in the evening he died of the beating and was buried in the cemetery of the camp. There were several dozen dead daily.

A year passed in this manner. Then the Germans announced that soldiers of Lithuanian citizenship could return home. By bribery, Leizer Stutsinsky obtained Lithuanian citizenship and returned to Eishishok.

Leizer's success made us all want to try our luck. On the second day after Stutsinsky had left the camp, when the German in charge of our row of huts asked which of the soldiers were Lithuanians, Meir Shimon Politatsky replied: "l am! I am an Eishishok native and Eishishok is part of Lithuania", " What is your name?", the German asked. " Meir Politatsky", he answered. " A Jew?" " Yes." " Good. Come with me Jude!" He was taken to a hut and left there. We did not know what happened to him and were extremely worried. In the evening, the door of our hut was opened and a body thrown inside. The body lay there on the ground, seemingly lifeless. Only when we bent over and looked into the face we recognized Meir Politatsky... he looked terrible. He was blue and swollen all over. His eyes were invisible for his face was swollen with wounds. We could barely revive him. He later became ill with epilepsy....Thus the Germans punished a Jew who " dared" request release from a prison camp. Meanwhile Lithuania was annexed to Russia. Lithuanian soldiers were no longer released and our last hope of escaping the Germans through that channel vanished.

From Germany we were taken to Poland to Biala Podlaska. Politatsky was released after the visit of a committee for the treatment of the ill. Berke Kaganovitz and I decided to escape the camp to one of the adjacent villages still inhabited by Jews. Jews were forbidden to use trains or buses but freedom of movement by carts or by foot was still permitted. Assisted by Belorussian soldiers who had some Christian acquaintances in the vicinity, we disguised ourselves as Jewish citizens, sewed the yellow patch on our clothes and thus reached Lukow. We there found work at a Jewish carpenter.

When Jews were ordered to work for German employers only, the Jewish carpenter found us work as apprentices in the carpentry of a German acquaintance in need of workers. The German was happy to find such cheap, nearly free, labour. I was an experienced carpenter and the German was very satisfied with my work. Thanks to him we escaped five " actions" (Jewish liquidation operations). When the number of Jews in Lukow dropped to a few dozen, the German told me: " Listen Jude, you've got to leave Lukow - they say that soon Lukow will be " Judenrein". I can't hide you any longer, and I feel sorry for you. You're a good worker and an honest Jew. Go to Mezritz, there are still many Jews there." We thanked him and Berke and I set off for Mezritz. The Jews and German supplied us with a little money and clothing. We hid in the forests by day and continued our journey by night. We were of course, disguised as Christian peasants and we obtained food from peasants on the way. On the third day we suddenly encountered a Polish policeman who demanded that we accompany him to the German police station in the nearby village for an investigation. We were in great danger.

The policeman did not believe we were Poles! We made a show of agreeing to go along with him but when we reached a thicket - Berke suddenly attacked him, grabbed his gun and killed him. We fled to the forest but having heard the shot, the Germans appeared, and seeing us running they began shooting at us. Berke was hit and he fell only a few metres away from the forest. He did not get up. I was luckier and managed to reach the forest. I ran with all my strength. The sun had meanwhile set and the Germans apparently did not want to follow me into the forest. All that night I ran. I entered another thicker and bigger forest and hid there for three days, living off forest berries. In the evening of the fourth day I left the forest and finally arrived to Mezritz. There I became friendly with a soldier prisoner serving as head of the Jewish police. He supervised the big store of murdered Jews' clothing and allowed me to sell to the peasants as many clothes as I liked, purchase weapons and go to the forests. At that time, partisan groups appeared but no one was allowed into the forest without weapons.

I collected some thousand rubles from the sale of clothes and purchased a revolver. The peasants had loads of weapons from when the Polish army had retreated. At that time a Jewish partisan messenger came to Mezritz to enlist Jews with weapons and take them to the forest. Since I possessed a revolver he took me along with ten other Jews. Our troop was headed by the partisan leader known by his nickname " Piri".

Our numbers increased. Many Russian prisoners transferred by train to Germany, jumped through the train windows or through holes they forced in the car floors and fled to the woods. Some of them succeeded in reaching the partisans uninjured. But there was a severe shortage of weapons. We decided to confiscate the pigs of rich peasants in nearby villages, distribute them among the poor peasants in exchange for information on which peasants had weapons. This plan worked successfully. We obtained not only guns and grenades but also machine guns. Our numbers reached 800, 300 of whom were Jewish. We obtained food from the villages in the order and amount we imposed on them. We assumed an increasingly military form. Service units such as cooking, sanitary, etc. were organized and we became bold enough to openly confront Germans stationed in the big villages. We were informed that a German troop of 15 men was at the Voronitz estate. The head of the estate was an S.S, officer, A troop of 40 partisans was dispatched and they surrounded the estate on all sides. It was an unexpected attack. The Germans were killed and their weapons taken. As time went on and our operations increased, we contacted Moscow. Airplanes were sent carrying supplies of weapons, food, radios, money, chocolate, etc. A group of saboteurs, headed by the renowned partisan "Uncle Petya", was organized to blow up bridges and destroy railroads.

Once I was sent, with two other Jews, on a sabotage mission. Our assignment was to blow up the train rail near a village about 40 km away from our base. At night we approached the village. From afar we heard sounds of music playing and dancing. We entered the first house at the outskirts of the village and the peasant there told us there were Germans in the village. We returned to the rail, dug a pit, placed the explosives and blew up the rail. We returned safely to the forest.

Such sabotage operations and surprise attacks on German stations in the villages or on military units on their way to and from the front, increased daily and the Germans were forced to transfer who battalions from the front to reinforce security of the railroads, roads and their guard stations.

But we did not only have the Germans on our hands. White Polish partisans appeared in the forests and they fought us with greater hatred than they fought the Germans. We fought back and gave them the treatment they deserved. Their hatred of the Jews and Communists was boundless. Any Jewish partisan captured was tortured to death. We too killed the White partisans when we caught them. Once when our troop was returning from a sabotage operation, and passing close by a village, they shot at us from an ambush. Piri, the head of our troop, was killed. We decided to teach them a lesson and make an example of them so others would be too afraid to try any tricks. At night some of our troops surrounded the village and set it on fire. Anyone trying to escape was shot and killed. No one survived from this village and no house remained standing.

The partisans war was a war of life and death. We took no prisoners-anyone captured was killed following interrogation. The Germans did the same when they caught a partisan. If one of us was severely wounded and it was impossible to carry him to the forest or save his life-he would shoot himself to avoid falling in the hands of the cruel enemy.

When the Russians returned in 1944 and liberated Poland, I joined the regular Red Army. I returned to Biala Podleaka and was there assigned as chief of the department of criminal offenders in the District Police. I served there for half a year till I felt that I could no longer stand being in Poland. The chief of Police hinted to me that I must leave for there were many complaints about me from the personal vengeance I took on the White Poles (of the "Armia-Krayova") and the other anti- Semetic hooligans who had showed excessive cruelty to the Jews under the German rule. I understood him. I also had a strong desire to leave Poland which was soaked in so much Jewish blood. In a Russian military car I crossed the border and entered Austria. From there I reached Italy and then Israel.

The committee of the soup kitchen for the poor and its staff of volunteers. It was founded during the German occupation in World War I (1916), and provided hot meals to hundreds of the city's poor in Eishishok.

[Page 82]

The White Partisan Attack on Eishishok

Alter Michelovsky

After Lithuania was annexed to Soviet Russia, I served for four months as Militia commander of Eishishok. When the Germans entered the town, I was of course forced to go into hiding for I did not manage to escape with the Red Army, as it was, much of the Red Army in Lithuania had fallen prisoner.

A few days after the Germans arrived, they caught Avraham Krishilov, Yehuda Lev Solominsky and his wife, Manos, son of Yosel Belechrovitz and nine other Jews, took them outside of the village and killed them.

I hid in the Jewish cemetery. At midnight I went to the house of Yehuda Mendel Kremen and knocked on the window. His wife came out, gave me 1000 roubles, some shirts and peasant's clothes and told me to escape quickly for I was being searched for high and low.

That same night, disguised as a peasant, I set out for Voronova, 24 Kilometers away from Eishishok. I arrived there safely. From there I went to my sister Mina who lived in Dzevinishok.

When all Dzevinishok Jews were ordered to move to the Voronova Ghetto, I returned to Voronova. On May 4, 1942, the Ghetto Jews were assembled in the marketplace at the center of the town. Bent on our knees, we remained there, with no food or water, from 8 a.m. to 3 p.m. Then, Lithuanian punitive troops came and divided the crowd into professionals and non-professionals. When I replied to the question of the police-chief that I was a watchmaker, he said "Well, for the time being you will live". I was told to stand on the right, while a huge crowd of non-professionals designated for slaughter, was gathered on the left... Before our very eyes the police- men attacked the crowd and displaying the barbarity of wild animals, seized the little money the Jews had, their rings, watches and other possessions. Meanwhile the peasants had finished digging the long pits. Then those unhappy people were forced to lie in the pits. Those who lagged behind or tried to resist were beaten with rifle butts and whips. When all the people in the pits were arranged "in the typical German order and methodology", they fired the machine guns positioned behind the Jews, and, their horrific rattle silences the cries of the Jews. The murdered and wounded Jews were covered with earth by the peasants. Puddles of blood spread over the whole market square around the awful pit, and we were standing there witnessing the scene. I will never, ever forget that awful sight.

When the slaughter was over, the Lithuanian district commander approached us and announced "All Jews are Communists and responsible for the war. Therefore they were killed. This will be the fate of all the Jews in Europe. You will remain alive for the time being. We have need of you !"

The survivors, amounting to 60-70 people, were led, on foot, to the Lida ghetto, which was strictly guarded by Germans and Lithuanians. The latter proved to be even crueler than the Germans.

Rumors had meanwhile spread that there were Jewish partisans in the nearby forest. A movement rose among the youth of the ghetto to steal out and reach the forests. We know that those who remained in the ghetto were doomed, be it to a slow or quick death, all would surely die! But without weapons no one was accepted in the woods. Partisan messengers succeeded in stealing into the ghetto and they began enlisting people. I bought a gun for 30,000 rubles from a young Christian boy who visited the Christian lady assigned the task of delivering the cakes baked in the ghetto for the S.S. officers. I dismantled the gun, hid its parts in my trousers and one dark night, by cutting the barbed wire surrounding the ghetto, escaped with 100 others to the woods. The wood we escaped to was the big Naliboky Forest, where, according to our information, the partisans headed by the brothers Beilski of Novogrodek were operating. During the day we hid in the forest and at night we continued our journey. We crossed the river Neiman not far from a German post and in the forest we met partisan guards of the Beilski group. We were brought to the camp and accepted as members. We all possessed weapons. In our camp there were several hundred partisans, all Jewish, among them women and children who prepared food, cleaned the clothes, and took care of the camp necessities.

Our assignments were attacks on solitary German and Lithuanian guards, exploding railroads and bridges and other acts of sabotage. Peasants found to be traitors or informers were liquidated. Food was received, or rather taken, from the peasants in the villages from which we operated. Our history during the more than two years spent in the forest is described in Beilski's book "The Jews of the Forests".

When the Russians returned, I went back to Eishishok. There I found Shalom Sonenson, his brother Moshe and his wife Zipporah and their children, the family of Zirl Yurkansky and Sara Kabatznik.

I enlisted in the N.K.V.D. troop which operated in Eishishok and the vicinity to purge the area of the Hitler collaborators and the White Polish partisans who we had learned to know during our "hot" "encounters" with them in the forests. Moshe Sonenson and myself, thirsty for revenge, belonged to an armed unit which, while pretending to search for Germans and traitors took reprisals on the evil Goys as they richly deserved.

We terrorized the Goys. We collected many articles and clothes robbed from Jews we had known and made those goys pay, if only a fraction, for what they had done to us and our children. We also caught Germans who had fled in small groups to the woods during the big retreat, and " framed" them. Once we captured six Germans, one of whom was an S.S. officer. Moshe Sonenson, myself and some other Jews took them to the cemetery where the Eishishok Jews had expired in terrible torture. We placed the officer to one side and told him: "You will remain alive!" "Yes, since I have a wife and sons in Germany", he said and a flicker of hope lit his extinguished eyes. The rest of the Germans stood pale, trembling with fear.

We did not prolong settling our account with them. A volley of bullets was fired and the contaminated bodies rolled on the ground by the big mass grave of our brothers. A small revenge for their crimes. " Now its your turn, dirty murderer", Moshe shouted. The officer was pallid with terror and realized that his end had come. He threw himself to the ground and started kissing the earth at our feet, crying and whimpering: "Good Jews! Pity me - I have a wife and children, I did you no wrong."

"You have a wife and children, do you?" Moshe shouted, "and we, didn't we have wives and children? You had no pity for our families and all that was clear to us- you filthy murderer! You want to live?! You won't live - you'll die like dogs!" While he was speaking he lifted his rifle butt and smashed the skull of the loathsome German. He then raised his hands , and cried in a terrible voice, " Here, my hands have spilled this defiled blood! For the sake of my father and mother, my brothers and sisters-for my baby son who was strangled by unhappy Jews—because of you, you murderers, you scum of the earth!..."

Thus, we continued to terrorize the "German collaborators" and those who had "enjoyed" the spectacle of Jewish murder. The Russian army had meanwhile left the village on its way west and only three militiamen remained in the village. Rumours reached us that a group of White Polish partisans were preparing to attack us while the Goys of the village were expectantly waiting for a sign to destroy us. We were informed that the attack was to be launched one night soon. These rumours reached us through those few Goys who had remained human and who welcomed with joy the return of the Jews, their good friends from before the war.

A Russian captain passed through Eishishok and we told him of the danger awaiting us and we requested that he dispatch troops of soldiers to the village. He tried to allay our fears by saying we had no reason to fear for our lives for under Russian rule such a predicament was impossible. He then continued on his way.

We all decided to gather in the house of Sonenson which was a brick house. That night the calamity struck, eight White Polish partisans, accompanied by a mass of the native Eishishok Goys, surrounded the house and started shooting. We defended ourselves bravely and prevented their approach. But we ran out of bullets and the crowd broke in the house. I jumped out the attic window to the garden behind the house. There I found Moshe, son of Marayshel Yurkansky, and we both fled to the river behind " Pigs' Street". All night we lay among the bushes. When morning came and the partisans had returned to the forests, we went back to the town and heard of the calamity. Moshe Sonenson, his wife Zipporah and their year old baby daughter were hiding in the room. They recognized the voices of some local Goys - the pharmacist, the medical aide, and others. Zipporah said: "I will go out and beg for our lives, they know us. The pharmacist used to come to our pharmacy. He was father's friend... Maybe they will have pity on us and our baby...They will find us here anyway!" Moshe agreed. No sooner had Zipporah opened the door and faced them, than they shot her and her baby, killing them on the spot. The Goys left the house after plundering and ravaging everything.

We ran to Radun and brought a troop of Soviet soldiers. A search was held in the Goys homes and we found many of our belongings. 50 were arrested, A few days later the partisans attacked the prison at night (the prison was the house of Kyuchevsky) and freed all the prisoners. All night there were gunshots between the attackers and the soldiers who dared not emerge from the house in which they were fortified.

Slowly, life returned to normal. Most of the houses were in one piece, though windows and doors were missing. Goys from "Pigs Street' or "Nyaar Plan" returned and occupied the better houses. Polish shops were opened and Polish craftsmen, tailors shoemakers, etc., came and replace the Jews that were gone. On Thursday, market day was held as usual. Peasants from the vicinity came to buy and sell and we often recognized the Jewish fur or coat they were wearing.

Our hearts ached to see how life went on even without the Jews as if the liquidation of the thousands of Jews, who had filled the village with their bargaining and love of life - was a normal and natural phenomenon!

We felt we could not return to the life as it had been. The hatred of the Goys for us was fierce and unconcealed and we decided to leave our home town - the town which was the cemetery of our dear and loved ones. The police officer also hinted to me that I should leave soon because the Goys were planning to prosecute us for " taking the law into our own hands" — which in Russia constituted a grave offense.

I did as the officer advised, I left Eishishok, went to Vilna and from there I crossed the border and made my way to Israel in the well-known way - the Haapala.

[Page 87]

Yiddish Section

Translated by Jerrold Landau

"… And here and there, from all the dark nooks ---
One sees eyes, eyes, silent eyes peer…
The souls of the martyrs are peering
Scattered, repressed souls -- -- --
Peer at you for a long time with silent eyes.
That only demand and ask without words
And complain in silence about all those old complaints,
That once again did not reach the heavens
And will never reach the heavens:
"Why? Why? And again Why???..."

(Ch. N. Bialik, "In the City of Slaughter")[1]

[Page 89]

The History of Eishishok
(A brief historical overview)

{Page 89 in Yiddish is equivalent with <u>page 3</u> of the Hebrew}

[Page 90]

The Jewish Community

{Page 90 and the top half of 91 in Yiddish is equivalent with <u>page 4</u> of the Hebrew.}

[Page 91]

The Economic and Cultural Life[2]

In former years, many Jews of Eishishok owned fields and pastures, and they were occupied with agriculture and gardening. In later years, after the land was taken away from them, they transferred to business and "industry" – that is shopkeeping and trades. Eishishok was known for its market and fairs. The Jews of the town lived like hundreds of thousands of other Jews in the Lithuanian-Polish cities and towns.

As has been stated, the economic situation became more difficult at the beginning of the 20th Century, and especially under Polish rule. As is known, the Polish regime sought any means to push the Jews out of their economic positions, and

[Page 92]

the Jews of Eishishok very quickly felt the anti-Semitic politics of that regime.

In the latter years, a merchants' union, a handworkers' union, and others were founded in the wake of the struggle with the politics of confrontation of the regime and the anti-Semitic incitement.

Cultural and Zionist-political activity had always taken a special place in societal life in Eishishok. Immediately after the advent of Zionism, a local group was founded by Yitzchak Wilkanski, the son of Rabbi Leizer the rabbinical judge (today a professor at the University of Jerusalem). In the later years, chapters of almost all of the Zionist factions (Poalei Zion, Hashomer Hatzair, Beitar, etc.) as well as pioneering [*chalutz*] groups from all ends of the spectrum were represented in town. We can state without exaggeration that during the last years before the Holocaust, all the youth of the town were involved in Zionist groups, and lovingly participated in all Zionist activities, as was the case in only few towns in Lithuania and White Russia.

The active Zionist work branched out into a very loving cultural activity, especially in the realm of Hebrew. After 1906, a youth organization Rak Ivrit [Only Hebrew] was founded in the town by Sara Wilkanski, which brought in almost all the youth. There, Hebrew became almost the second mother tongue of the youth. Already a decade previously, theater was performed in Eishishok in Hebrew, and lectures in Hebrew were a daily occurrence. However, not only in Hebrew – cultural life in Yiddish was also very regular, and Eishishok was justly considered one of the culturally active towns in Lithuania.

Translator's Footnotes:

1.   A full translation of this poem, albeit not an exact translation of the original, can be seen at: https://www.wzo.org.il/index.php?dir=site&page=articles& op=item&cs=3140&category=3032&language=eng. My translation is more literal, and less poetic.
2.   This article is a very brief summary of topics covered at length in the Hebrew sections from pages 27-44.

[Page 93]

The Destruction of Eishishok

The Destruction of Eishishok

As told by Eishishok refugees

Translated by Jerrold Landau

We present here the tragic history of the destruction of Eishishok, as told by Jews of Eishishok whose fate it was to survive and arrive in the Land of Israel. Everything that they tell us is the pure truth, without exaggeration. We present here their memoirs and experiences exactly as they have related to us – in their style and their form – barely changing a single word...

Translator's note:

The following five Holocaust testimonies were expected to be equivalent in Hebrew and Yiddish. The analogous Hebrew testimonies start on page 57. Although the substance of the testimonies are largely equivalent, the Hebrew and Yiddish text differ slightly, both with respect to nuance to facts. Since these were intended to be equivalent, I assume that the differences were introduced in translating the original Yiddish text into Hebrew (though it is possible that it was vice-versa) in the original book. The original translator likely amended some of the facts. For this reason, a decision was made to fully translate the Yiddish versions of these testimonies.

The Last Days of Eishishok

Related by Shalom Sonenson (Ben-Shemesh)[1]

On September 17, 1939, Soviet tanks and other motorized military apparatus entered Eishishok. A Revkom (Revolutionary Committee) was immediately set up town. The Eishishker Communist Chaim Shuster was installed as leader. The first order of the Revkom was the ban on any Zionist activity. All Zionist organizations were immediately closed. The Hebrew School turned into a Yiddishist school]. The merchandise in the shops

[Page 94]

was immediately confiscated, and inflation increased. However, the Soviet regime in the town did not last for long. One month later, Eishishok and the entire Vilna region was given over by the Soviets to the "independent" Lithuanian republic, and a Lithuanian regime was installed in the town. Life once again began to flow normally. The shops were again full of all sorts of merchandise. The Zionist organizations were again active, and the school again became a Hebrew school.

Hundreds and thousands of refugees from the parts of Poland that were under the Soviet regime, and even from Western Poland where the Nazis ruled, passed through Eishishok. Eishishok was near the Russian-Lithuanian border. (The border was at the village of Tavshiun [Tausiūnai], four kilometers from Eishishok.) From Eishishok, they went to Vilna, the capital of Lithuania, which was a large Zionist center at that time. From Vilna, it was still possible to travel to the Land of Israel or other countries.

In Eishishok, a refugee committee was founded, which was mainly involved in assisting the refugees with the Lithuanian police, who would send them back to the Russian side. The committee would save them from the hands of the Lithuanians, and provide them with food and dwelling for a few days, until they could be sent to Vilna. It was not only the committee, but all Eishishoker Jews, almost without exception, who displayed their brotherly dedication. Nothing was too hard for them to help the refugees. Eishishok was the bright point in their long, painful wandering[2]. In the summer of 1940, after the Lithuanian Republic

[Page 95]

"voluntarily" united with Soviet Russia, the situation of the Jews in Lithuania in general, and in Eishishok in particular, took a significant turn for the worse.

The Communists again took over the regime, and this time for a lengthy period. The Communists who fled in 1939 returned to Eishishok and became the bosses again, with greater boldness. The Zionist organizations were again closed. The school again became Yiddishist-Communist. The businesses of Kopelman, Weidenberg, Kiuchewski, Abelow, and others were confiscated. A Communist party was formed with Lipke Ginunski as the head, as was a Komsomol (Communist Youth Organization) with Reuvele, the son of Shmuel the shoemaker, as the chairman.

Illegal business blossomed, ignoring all the fines and confiscations, and people "made money." This is how people lived under the Soviet-Lithuanian regime until the outbreak of the Russian-German war on June 22, 1941.

The Nazis were already in Eishishok on June 24, the day after the outbreak of the war. Things were calm in the town during the first few weeks, as long as the German army was streaming through the town to the front in the east. Jews remained in their houses behind closed doors and shutters. Their hearts palpitated with terror when they heard the bangs and noise from the innumerable tanks and autos on the highway. When the noise stopped, and the army stopped streaming through the town, a division of the TODT-Arbeits-Amt remained. They enlisted all the men between the ages of 16 and 60 to work at repairing the highway that led from Eishishok to Vilna. The workday was 14 hours, from 7:00 a.m.

[Page 96]

until 9:00 p.m. Given that the workplace was for the most part 10 kilometers from the town, they had to present themselves at 5:00 a.m. and they returned around 11:00 p.m. The wages were 50 pfennig a day. The guard consisted of elderly Germans who were called Volksdeutschen – that is, Polish citizens of German extraction, who declared themselves as German citizens at the beginning of the Polish-German war. These new "apostates" displayed greater hatred and cruelty to the Jews and Poles than did the true Germans. After a difficult workday, tired and hungry, the Volksdeutschen would conduct "military exercises" with the Jews. That is, they would strip them naked and make them fight with each other, etc. They were murderously beaten for every minor infraction, without differentiation between old and young.

Another division of younger murderers arrived at the beginning of the second month. The commandant summoned the rabbi, Rabbi Shimon Rozovski, of blessed memory, and ordered him to form a Jewish committee of 12 individuals, who would be responsible for the precise and immediate fulfilment of their commands. The rabbi summoned all men of the town to the synagogue to select the committee. However, since there were no "takers" for such an "honor", they decided to cast lots to select the 12 members. According to the lot, Avraham Kaplan was selected as chairman, Shalom Soneson as vice chairman, Yehuda Dwilanski, Yehuda Sewicki, Itza Mendel Jurkonski, Yosef Michalowski, Chanan Michalowski, Mordechai Kaganowicz, Markl Kopelman, and Efraim Karnowski were selected.

A few days later, the Nazis commanded to bring all fineries, jewelry, gold and silver rings, furs, and other valuable items to the kommandator (in Kiuczewski's house). All this

[Page 97]

was packed in large crates and sent to the fatherland – Germany. New orders were issued every day, one worse than the other. For every minor delay – beatings and other sadistic tortures.

One Sabbath, the murderers captured a few hundred Jews with long beards, placed them in two rows, brought them to the river on Vilner Way, and ordered them to enter the water in their clothes. Then, they unfortunate people had to roll along the highway in their wet clothing to clean the highway from dust. Then, they sicced their wild dogs upon the Jews, and the Jews emerged barely alive, bitten and wounded by the Nazis and the dogs. They were barely able to run to the first Jewish houses on Vilner Street[3]. The Nazis displayed their sadistic inclinations by destroying the bath and the *mikveh*. They broke the gravestones in the cemetery, and the they took the *parochets* [ark curtains], lamps, and chandeliers from the *Beis Midrashes*. They broke the benches. The "bearers of culture" publicly burned the books from the city library and the *Beis Midrashes*.

The situation became more serious when the de-facto authority over the Jews in the town was given over to the Lithuanian police, headed by Astrauvskas, who was known as a murderer and a sadist. The Lithuanian police overtook their German teachers in their bloodthirstiness, anti-Semitism, and bestiality…

In the meantime, rumors reached us about the murder of entire Jewish communities in Lithuanian towns. Gentiles would secretly come to their Jewish acquaintances and tell them about the tragic end of the Jews of Lithuania, and advised them to give over the bit of property that they still had – "for in any case, they will kill you. Your end is near, and

The market in Eishishok on a Thursday (1912)

[Page 98]

nothing will save you." They ended with a sigh, apparently out of sympathy.

Nevertheless, despite everything, we hoped that the misfortune would not come to us. We wanted to live, and every illusion was stronger than the terrible reality. We believed privately that we would survive the terrible times and our enemies. Some of us indeed would be killed, but the majority would survive. Everyone wanted to believe that he would be among the survivors...

We did not want to believe all the terrible rumors. "It is certainly overstated"... the optimists among us would comfort themselves, and they were the vast majority... "The gentiles are deliberately exaggerating so that they can trick us out of the little bit that we have... They will not kill thousands of Jews! They only want our money!" – thus did they comfort themselves and did not believe the gentiles.

A few days before Rosh Hashanah 5702 (September 21-23, 1941), a trustworthy gentile came and told us that he was in the town of Aran [Varėna] and saw hundreds of Jewish corpses lying around... and that the German and Lithuanian police are preparing to do the same thing in all the Lithuanian cities and towns.

Then the rabbi, Rabbi Shimon Rozovski of blessed memory, called a clandestine meeting of the important householders of the town, and told them, "Jews, our final hour is near, the murderers are preparing for our slaughter. Let us at least die with honor. Let us purchase some weapons with the last bit that we have. If our fate is to die, let it at least be with weapons in our hand. Let my soul die with the Philistines!"[4]. However, Yosel Weidenberg was opposed:

"You want to fight with the Germans? Who and what are we? They want

[Page 99]

only our money. Let us give it to them. They do not want to kill an entire city! Let us attempt to bribe the commandant! We must not risk the life of an entire city!"

The opinions were counted, and the meeting resulted in nothing.

Many Jews gave over valuables to good and well-known Christians in the villages. When the rabbi heard this, he forbade people from doing so. "You are thereby making the gentiles your worst enemies, for they will be the first to want to be freed from you," he claimed. However, they did not listen to him. Everyone wanted to be secure, and believed "their" gentile.

On Sunday, the eve of Rosh Hashanah 5702 [1941], all the Jews, regardless of age of weakness, even the ill, were gathered into the two *Beis Midrashes* and the large synagogue. Anyone who was found in a house or in hiding would be shot on the spot.

A terrible panic overtook the entire city. Now, everyone understood the intention of the murderers. People began to seek places to hide, or ways to flee from the town...

However, it was already too late. The city was surrounded by the Lithuanian police. Nevertheless, approximately 490 people succeeded in evading the police via the hills and escaping to the forests.

My wife, our two young children, and I also succeeded in hiding in a lumber warehouse. At 8:00 p.m., when it was very dark, we snuck out of the lumber workshop. Since our house was at the edge of the town, we snuck through the fields and ran to the Senadvaris Forest.

[Page 100]

There we met Shlomo Kiuczewski, his brother-in-law Yefim Schipel, Reuven Kaleko and family, Leib Kowenski and his father, and Ita Sziszka (a women over 80). We divided into two groups. One went toward Voronovo, and the second, I among them, went to Radun. Both of those towns belonged to the White Russian region – and the murderous Lithuanian police were not there. There, Jews were still able to move about and travel.

When we arrived in Radun, we met Jews of Eishishok who told us about the last days of the Eishishok community:

... All the Jews of Eishishok, along with those of Olkeniki [Valkininkai], who had been brought in a day earlier, approximately 4,000 individuals, were prodded into the two *Beis Midrashes* and the synagogue. They were held there for three days without food and water. They even had to attend to the call of nature on the spot... On Wednesday, Tzom Gedalia [The fast of Gedalia, the day after Rosh Hashanah], they were all brought to the new horse market on Raduner Street under the guard of the Lithuanian and German police. The Jews were placed into rows, and they recited the confessional with weeping and screaming, led by Cantor Tiwalski.

On Thursday, Tishrei 4 in the morning, the Lithuanian police commandant – the murderer Astrauvskas – chose 250 young, healthy men and sent them to an unknown direction.

Then, I found out that they brought them to the old cemetery, where they were shot by the Lithuanian police and tossed into the large graves that the gentiles had dug a few days earlier. 250 people were sent every hour. In order to calm the outraged Jews, a Lithuanian policeman

[Page 101]

brought a note signed by Leib Milikowski that "We are now on Seklotzky's yard, and are preparing a ghetto for you. Have no fear, we are awaiting your arrival."

The little note that Milikowski wrote under duress encouraged the sworn optimists somewhat, and the Jews went to their slaughter without knowing the truth. The next day, 5 Tishrei, they took the men and children, and by Friday afternoon, not one of the Jews of Eishishok and Olkeniki was alive, other than the few who succeeded in sneaking away or escaping.

The murderer Astrauvskas, dressed in a white apron and white gloves, shot the Jewish children with his own hands. The final victim was the rabbi, Rabbi Shimon Rozovski, may the memory of the holy be blessed, whom the murderers held in the cemetery for both days so that he would see how his community was destroyed. Immediately after the slaughter, the murderer relived the unfortunate man of his pain with a bullet from his revolver. The devoted rabbi found his final rest in the common grave of the 4,000 martyrs of the communities of Eishishok and Olkeniki.

Translator's Footnotes:

1.   The author is the uncle of the Eishishok native and well-known historian, teacher, and author Prof. Yaffa Eliach (1935-2016), who wrote *There Once Was a World: A 900-Year Chronicle of the Shtetl of Eishyshok* (1998).
2.   There is a footnote in the text here: See the article in the Hebrew section, pages 47-55.
3.   Editor: This probably is Vilniaus gatvė – Vilnius Street.
4.   Judges 16:30.

In the Bunkers

Related by Yaffa Sonenson[1]
(The ten-year-old daughter of Moshe Sonenson)

Translated by Jerrold Landau

When the Lithuanian police began to drive the Jews out of the *Beis Midrashes*, my older brother Yitzchak and I were hiding in a hut for storing lumber. We lay there until it was quite dark. My father had escaped a day

[Page 102]

earlier, but my mother with my young brother who was still nursing did not succeed in hiding, and were brought to the *Beis Midrashes* by the wicked ones. At night, we crawled out from the stored wood, and escaped through the yards to Yashka Eliaskewicz, a Christian who had worked in our tannery for many years. Our father had told us to go there in the event of danger. With him, we found David Mashcenik's children, Myra and her brother Meir, and several other Jews.

The following afternoon, a gentile came to us, sent by our father to bring us to the village of Dumblya [Polish: Dumbla; Lithuanian: Dumblė]. We dressed up as Christian children, and the gentile brought us to a house in Dumblya. There, we found our father and our relative Sara Kabacznik and her family.

We spent five days with the Christian acquaintance, and then we decided to go to Vasilishki, where Jews still lived. The police commandant, a Pole, was a great anti-Semite. When our father came to the police station to present himself, as the law demanded (otherwise, our Jewish acquaintance would be afraid to host us), the police commandant ordered that Father be arrested, because he had traveled from Lithuania to White Russia[2] without a permit.

Once, the commandant saw me bringing Father a bottle of milk. He grabbed the bottle from my hands and broke it, shouted at me to go away, and told me to never again approach the jail. Father was freed from jail after ten days thanks to a large bribe. A few days later we received news from a Christian that Mother and my young brother were alive, and they were in Radun. We immediately set out for Radun

[Page 103]

and found them there. They were saved at the last moment. When the police drove them into the *Beis Midrashes* along with other Jews, they took the opportunity and escaped through a side door. With the help of a Christian acquaintance, they left the town dressed as Christians. The Christian returned to her home. Suddenly Mother saw a policeman approaching her. Realizing that they had seen her escaping, Mother began to walk slower. To her good fortune, there were still large piles of hay lying in the fields. She tossed my little brother into a pile of hay, and hid herself in a second pile of hay. The police did not see anything, and thought that she had disappeared into the forest, so they returned to Eishishok. That is how they were saved.

We lived in Radun for several months. During that time, the Germans set up a ghetto in Radun as well. We and 16 other Jews hid in an attic. We did not want to enter the ghetto.[3] Suddenly, my brother started to cry. Mother let him nurse, but the child did not stop crying. He cried stronger and stronger.

A death pall fell upon us all. Then an elderly Jew called out to Mother: "This child will get us all killed. Sixteen lives are more valuable than the life of a child. He must be silenced." The man took a blanket and thew it upon the child. After a few moments, the child was silenced forever... Mother fainted... Everyone remained sitting frozen.

It was calm for a few days. We escaped to the village of Korkutsyany. A gentile acquaintance agreed to hide us for a large sum of money. He dug a large pit in his pigsty. He covered the pit with boards.

[Page 104]

He then covered the boards with manure, and placed on top an old sack, potatoes, and other things. My parents, my brother Yitzchak, a female relative from Olita, and I "lived" in that pit. Our food consisted of only potatoes that the gentile would give us through a secret hole. We never saw the sunshine throughout that time. Our money began to run out, and we could not pay the "inflated" prices for the bit of potatoes that he would give us, so the gentile ordered us to leave his "dwelling." If we would not, he would turn us over to the Germans. We returned to the village of Lebedyanka [Polish: Lebiedniki; Belarusian: Lebedniki (Лябеднікі)] and again lived in a pit for a year. We found our uncle Shalom Sonenson with his daughter Gitele in Lebedyanka. A year later, the peasant became more brazen, and demanded more money, so we decided to go out to the partisans.

We lived for about two years with the partisans, and endured many tribulations and dangers. When the Russians returned in 1944, we came out from the forests and returned to Eishishok. However, we did not find any peace there either. The White Polish partisans[4] shot my Mother and little brother during the great attack against the Jews in the town. My father was sentenced [by the Soviets] to eight years in Siberia. The gentiles falsely accused that he had conducted business without a permit. My brother Yitzchak remained in Russia to try to arrange my father's release. I arrived in the Land of Israel with my Uncle Shalom, and I wait impatiently for my father and brother to be together with me in the Land of Israel.

Editor's Footnotes:

1.   The author was the Eishishok native and well-known historian, teacher, and author Prof. Yaffa Sonenson Eliach (1935-2016), who wrote *There Once Was a World: A 900-Year Chronicle of the Shtetl of Eishyshok* (1998).

2.   On September 1, 1939, Nazi Germany invaded Poland but its forces only seized the western half of the country. On September 17, 1939, the Soviet Union took control of the eastern half of Poland (the "Kresy"). In October 1939, the Soviets transferred the Vilna / Wilno / Vilnius region to Lithuania and the rest of the Kresy was annexed to the Soviet Union's puppet state of Byelorussia ("White Russia," today, Belarus). A person who did not reside in the Soviet Union needed a visa to enter the country.

3.   At the beginning of the Holocaust in Lithuania and Belarus, the Nazis and their local paramilitary forces would designate the poorest part of a town as a "ghetto" – an urban concentration camp – and ordered all other Jews living in the town and surrounding area to live there. The author's family was apparently hiding in the attic of a house that was outside of the "ghetto."

4.   The term "White Polish partisans" refers to underground forces that opposed both the Nazi and the Soviet occupiers of territory that had been part of Poland before September 1939.

[Page 105]

The life of Jewish "forest-people"

Told by Rachel Futcher

Translated by Jerrold Landau

When the Germans seized control of Eishishok in July 1941, the economic and societal life came to a halt. The shops were closed. The *Beis Midrashes* were empty. Jews did not dare to go out on the streets, even though at that time it was permitted to do so, but, of course only in the ditches and not on the sidewalks, and wearing the "yellow patch" on their chest and on their shoulders. People only went out for the most necessary reasons, such as fetching water from a well or purchasing food. No market took place. Gentiles were forbidden to do business with Jews. There was no shortage of food. Everyone had prepared large reserves of food during the time of the Soviet regime. Flour, potatoes, sugar, and other foodstuffs could be found in almost every house. The poor people would receive support from the Jewish Committee.

This is the way it was for the first few months. Terrible rumors regarding mass murder in the surrounding towns began to reach us via Christian acquaintances, who met with Jews and gave over the news.

This was the way it was until the final Sunday of the eve of Rosh Hashanah 5702 [1941]. All the Jews were driven by the Lithuanian and German police to the two *Beis Midrashes* and the synagogue. They held us there for up to three days.

On Monday, the first day of Rosh Hashanah, a Lithuanian policeman entered the new *Beis Midrash*, where I, my husband, and our two sons were also found. He called Avraham Szwarc and ordered him to come with him. The policeman ordered Szwarc to take him to

[Page 106]

his house. The policeman told Szwarc that [supposedly] a large sum of money, belonging to him and to the Jewish community, was hidden in a secret place in Szwarc's house, and that if Szwarc did not voluntarily tell the policeman where the money was Szwarc would pay with his life. Avraham Szwarc swore that this was nothing more than a frame-up by gentile haters, and that there was nothing in his house. However, none of Avraham Szwarc's denials that he had not hid any money helped him. When the policeman saw that he would not get anything from Szwarc, the policeman took him to the new cemetery and shot him. Then, the policeman came once again to the *Beis Midrash*, and ordered Avraham's brother, David Szwarc, to go to the cemetery to bury his brother. We sat in the *Beis Midrash* for two days without food or drink. On Wednesday, the Fast of Gedalia, they removed everybody from the two *Beis Midrashes*, arranged them in lines, and led us to the new horse market on Raduner Street under guard by Lithuanian policemen. The next day, they first chose the youngest and strongest men, and sent them in an unknown direction. From afar, we heard the shooting of guns, but even then we did not believe that they were leading them to slaughter. We hoped that they were going to make a ghetto for us. We believed that the shooting was only meant to scare us, or perhaps it was a game by the murderers. We did not want to believe that the last hour was approaching. We wanted to live – to live under any condition...

They led away all the men throughout the day. By evening, only women and children remained in the horse market. Night fell. The thousands of women and children lay on the cold ground, more dead than alive, and waited for the next day...

In the middle of the night, I heard a board from the fence (the horse

[Page 107]

market was then surrounded by boards) moving to the side, and in the silence a recognizable voice spoke to me in Polish. This was a gentile who we knew well, who took a risk in the dark night to sneak in among the women.

"Tomorrow they will shoot you, just as they have shot your husbands. Escape from death – if your life is still worthwhile to you. Escape while it is not too late. Tomorrow will be late, too late!"

I and my two sons (my husband had been shot in the morning) along with Itke Konichowski and her two children, Shoshke Jurkanski and her son, who were lying in one corner, decided to follow the advice of the peasant. We quietly crawled through the area of the board that had moved, and went with the peasant to an acquaintance of hers in Duchishok [Dotishki]. After a few days, we sent the peasant to see what had happened in Eishishok. When the peasant returned, we found out about the great disaster... Eishishok was Judenrein...

A few days later, I set out to my aunt in Beneyki. Chaikl Konichowski also went there with his wife Gittel and children.

When an order was given that all Jews in the region must gather in the Voranava Ghetto, I decided to not go to Voranava.

My heart told me that Voranava was simply a trap, and that the ghetto – meant death. Despite the desire of my family, I decided to disguise myself as a gentile woman and return to the area of Eishishok to hide with gentile acquaintances. That is what I did. Near Eishishok, I met a peasant acquaintance. I

[Page 108]

explained to him what I wanted and requested his help. The good peasant reassured me, and asked me to bring my sons from Beneyki. He promised to hide us. I returned to Beneyki, brought the children, and arrived at the peasant. Since the peasant was a soltys [chairperson of the village council], and German and Lithuanian police would come to his house, he was afraid of keeping us further. One could receive the death penalty for hiding Jews! That was the "law"!

What could we do now? The ground was already frozen, and snow began to fall. It was then then end of November. Where do we go now? Then I remembered that I had a few good gentile acquaintances in the village of Jurkiškė. Perhaps they would help us. I convinced the gentile to at least accompany us to Jurkiškė and show us from afar the house in which my acquaintance lives. I did not want to enter the house of an anti-Semitic gentile by mistake. The gentile agreed. We set out on our way on Saturday morning. We went through forests and fields. Finally, we arrived in the village. The peasant showed me the house of the acquaintance, and returned to his village. I knocked on the door. To my good fortune, my Christian acquaintance came out. When she saw me, she shrieked, "Jesus, Maria, is that you? I heard that you were also shot together with all the Jews of Eishishok?"

She took me into the house and said:

"I cannot keep you in the house. You see that my house is near the main road. Police pass by very often. I will take you to my sister. She lives in an isolated house deep in the forest. You can be hidden there. My sister will know how to be quiet.

Of course, I agreed, and late at night

[Page 109]

we arrived at her sister's house. The peasant woman received us in a friendly manner, and gave us a separate room in which we had to remain through the entire day, not showing ourselves to anyone. However, gentiles began to talk that Jews were hiding with her. We had to leave the house, and dig a pit one meter deep and two meters wide. We entered the pit through the hollow of a tree. We moved the roots aside and placed them over the opening of the pit. We could enter the pit through the hole. We "lived" in that "dwelling" for nine months. We received food from the Christian.

During that time we met a Russian soldier who was also hiding in the forest. We eventually became very friendly with him, and he would help us obtain food. After some time, White Polish partisans appeared in the forest, who fought against the "Reds" and the Jewish partisans as if against the Germans. A Jew who fell into their hands would not come out alive. The situation deteriorated, and we decided to join the partisans. My oldest son decided to try his luck and to find them. After many difficulties and dangers, he met a group of partisans in a forest. After telling them about our situation and our request, the leader of the group agreed to accept us into the partisans, and gave him a note. We crawled out of our pit in February 1944 and set out on our way. We almost fell into the hands of a White Polish partisan group, but we escaped from them with G-d's help and met a Red Partisan intelligence group. They did not want to take us in, because we

[Page 110]

had no weapons or money with us. They did not pay attention to the fact that we had the note from the partisan leader that my son had brought with him. They did agree to take my older son, but not me and my younger son. They did not permit us to go deeper into the forest to the partisan camp. Returning from where we had come would have been a certain death. What should we do? I decided to not move from the place. I placed my packages down on the snow and told them that we had nowhere else to go. If they wanted, they could shoot us.

We lay on the snow in that manner for six days until an order came from the high commander of the partisans to allow us into the forest and accept us to the partisans. I worked in the kitchen and was useful to them. My older son was taken into the intelligence division, and my younger son was taken into the pioneer division. To our good fortune, Russian airplanes dropped a great deal of weapons a few days earlier, and therefore they allowed us into the camp without concern that we came without weapons or money, thereby breaking the "partisan law" that "without weapons and without money, you cannot be a partisan." We spent a half a year with the partisans, and endured all the dangers of a life of wandering, until the Russians returned in July 1944 and liberated our area.

From the partisans, we went to Vilna, and were witnesses to the final battles between the Russian and German soldiers. From Vilna, we traveled to Eishishok, and lived there with the survivors, until the great attack of the White Polish partisans, who killed Feigele Sonsenson and her child. My son was also badly wounded

[Page 111]

in the foot by the White Polish partisans as he was traveling to Vilna. Despite all efforts, he died in Łódź a year later after great suffering.

Then, I decided to leave Poland. After many more difficulties, I and my younger son arrived in the Land of Israel in 1946 with the so-called "Second Aliya."

From a Prison Camp to a Partisan Life

Told by Shneur Glembocki

Translated by Jerrold Landau

When the Polish-German war broke out, I was mobilized as a soldier in Vilna.[1] Our regiment, along with several other regiments, was placed on trains and sent to the western front. After three days, I arrived in Siedlce, not far from Warsaw. Along the way, we already encountered various units of the defeated Polish army fleeing eastward. The disorder was indescribable. Every regiment, or more properly, every company, worried about itself and went where they wanted. The military command structure had already ceased functioning on the first day of the war. The German Luftwaffe had gained unchallenged rule of the skies. The army was full of traitors, and a "fifth column" sowed disorder and panic within the military chain of command. Entire armies were surrounded by the German armies. Soldiers cast down their weapons, which lay around everywhere. My company, which consisted of about 200 men, decided to return to their homes in the Vilna region. On the way back, we were captured and were brought

[Page 112]

to Siedlce. Thousands of Polish officers and soldiers were in the prison camp, hungry and worn out. Among them were some who had been seriously wounded, whose shrieks and groans filled the air. The hunger, cold, and disgraceful downfall of the Polish army aroused anti-Semitic instincts within the Poles, and they began to harass the Jewish soldiers. The Germans did not mix into the internal life of the prison camp, and the Polish hooligans had a free hand. A few weeks later, they brought us to a place near Königsberg,[2] and turned us over to the hands of the Volksdeutschen. These "guards," together with the Polish hooligans, attacked us and stole our property and the few "possessions" that we had with us. A few weeks later, we were placed in cattle cars and taken to a village called [Klein] Deksin. We went to the prisoner camp by foot. Along the way, we passed a German farm. A German child was standing at the fence holding two apples. Berke Kaganowicz, who was together in the row with me, ran out from the row, and grabbed the two apples from the *shegetz*, and ran back between the rows. The *shegetz* began to shriek, but he did not recognize the "robber" among the hundreds of prisoners. Berke, Yona Tawszunski, and I divided the two apples among ourselves.

This was the only food we had for two days. We arrived in the camp after two hours of walking. There was a German "sanitation committee" at the gate. A sanitation officer gave us an injection with ink as a protection against typhus...

[Page 113]

Our work consisted of cleaning the snow from the streets or building barracks. The workday spanned from 6:00 a.m. until 6:00 p.m. Our food was 200 grams of bread per day, on occasion a bit of margarine, and at noon a bowl of vegetable soup, of course without fat. Jews had to do the most difficult and dirtiest work.

In the prison camp, I met Leizer Stotszinski, Meir Shimon Politacki, the photographer Leibowicz, and Shaul Lidski's son. The Nazis administered death blows for every minor "infraction." Yona Tawszunski fell as a victim to the German beatings, and was buried in the cemetery of the prison camp. When the Germans ordered that Polish soldiers who had lived in the territory that Soviet Russia transferred to Lithuania were allowed to return to their places,[3] Leizer Stotszinski "obtained" Lithuanian citizenship and returned to Eishishok.

A few days later, after Leizer Stotszinski left the camp, the German in charge of our barracks asked the prisoners if any of them were Lithuanian citizens. Meir Shimon Politacki responded, "I! I am an Eishishoker, and Eishishok now belongs to Lithuania." The Nazi asked, "Where is your family?"

"Politacki! – A Jew? Ya! Good! Come with me, Jew!"

Meir Shimon did not return by evening. Suddenly, the door of our barracks opened, and a person was tossed at us. When I bent down to see who it was, I could barely recognize Politacki. He was one large wound. I could not see either of his eyes. His face was blue and swollen. We were able to revive him only with difficulty.

[Page 114]

From that time, [as a result of the severe beating he received,] he developed epilepsy. This is how the murderers punished Jews for the brazenness of wanting to be freed from their hands. Later, a health commission freed him from the camp.

From Germany, they brought us again to Biała Podlaska in Poland. Ber Kaganowicz and I dressed up in civilian Jewish garb, with the yellow batch on the chest and shoulders. We went in that manner to Łuków, and were taken on as workers by a Jewish carpenter.

Then, we worked for a German carpenter who treated us very humanely, and hid us from aktions – that means from being sent to the death camps.

When the situation became more serious, I dressed up as a Christian and set out for Międzyrzec, where a Jewish community still existed.

On the way, we encountered a Polish policeman who demanded that we go with him to the nearest police station to inspect our papers. He suspected that we were not Poles! Having no choice, we agreed to go with him. However, when we passed by a grove, Berke suddenly took out his gun and shot the policeman on the spot. We began to run quickly to the grove. The echo of the shot alerted the closest German guard and drew his attention. Seeing from afar two men running, the guard began to shoot. Berke fell a few meters from the grove, after having been hit by a German bullet. Thus did he meet his tragic death there.

My fate was better. I succeeded in running to

[Page 115]

the grove, and thus saved myself. Apparently, the Germans had no great desire to follow me into the grove, and since it was already quite dark, they returned to the village. I hid deep in the forest for three days. I finally arrived in Międzyrzec in the evening of the fourth day. In Międzyrzec, I formed a brotherly relationship with the Jewish police commandant. Thanks to him, I was able to obtain things from murdered Jews and sell them to the surrounding peasants. With the money I purchased a revolver.

At that time, a secret emissary of the Jewish partisans, who were moving about in the surrounding forests, arrived. I was accepted into the partisans along with another ten lads of Międzyrzec. We began to confiscate pigs from the wealthy peasants and distribute them among those in the village who had weapons.

Thanks to this, we not only purchased guns and revolvers, but even machine guns. With time, our numbers reached 800. We were divided into different companies and groups, including the sanitary, scouting, and other support groups.

With time, we made radio contact with Moscow, and from there we received weapons, radios, food, etc., from airplanes.

Our task was primarily to destroy bridges and railway lines, and to attack the German guard posts or military units that would pass through our area going to and from the front. We forced the Germans to dedicate large army units to fight against us. This restricted their freedom of movement and badly damaged their transport and communication networks.

[Page 116]

In the middle of the night, we suddenly attacked a village in which there was a German guard post. After carrying out the bit of work – we quickly disappeared... White Polish partisans appeared in the forests during the years 1942-1943. We endured the most bitter battles with them. Any Jewish partisan who fell into their hands would not come out alive. It was the same thing when we captured a white partisan. The partisans did not take any prisoners; therefore, every partisan knew that he must kill the enemy or he himself would be killed! If a partisan was badly wounded and it was impossible to take him along, the wounded partisan would shoot himself to avoid falling into the hands of the enemy, and meeting his death with suffering and pain.

One night, when my company passed near a village, guns started shooting at us. Since we knew that there were no Germans in the village, we understood that those who were shooting were peasants who were collaborating with the white Polish partisans. Then fell our beloved commander, who was known by the name "Piri." We decided to teach the village a lesson, so that it would serve as an example to others.

The following night, several groups surrounded the village and set it on fire from all sides. Anyone trying to escape was shot. No living person remained in the village.

Thus did I live a partisan life in the Polish forests for two years. When the Russian army liberated the Polish regions, I enlisted in the Red Amy, returned to Biała Podlaska, and in time became a prison

[Page 117]

commissar over criminals. As time went on, a significant number of anti-Semitic criminals and murderers of Jews were appropriately punished. About a half a year later, I felt that it was time to resign – too many complaints had been made against me. At the same time, I wanted to free myself from Poland and its human-beasts. I crossed the Russian-Austrian border in a Russian military vehicle. I arrived in the Land of Israel through the Ma'apilim route in the spring of 1946.[4]

Translator's Footnotes:

1.   During the inter-war period, 1920-1939, Vilna was under the control of the Second Polish Republic. On September 1, 1939, Nazi Germany invaded the western half of Poland.
2.   At the end of the Second World War, the city was renamed Kaliningrad.
3.   On September 17, 1939, the Soviet Union invaded the eastern half of Lithuania. Once the Polish state capitulated, the Nazis and Soviets distributed the territory of the Poland. On October 10, 1939, the Soviets agreed to transfer the Vilna region to the Republic of Lithuania.
4.   A Ma'apil (plural, Ma'apilim) is a Jew who immigrated illegally to pre-state Israel in violation of British rule in the 1930s and 1940s - Aliyah Bet.

The Attack of the White Partisans Upon Eishishok

Told by Alter Michalowski

Translated by Jerrold Landau

As a former commander of the Eishishok militia under the Soviet regime, I had to hide immediately after the entry of the Germans. I did not succeed in escaping with the retreating Russian army. I disguised myself as a peasant and managed to evade the German police, who were searching for me. I escaped to Varanava. On May 4, 1942, the German-Lithuanian police drove all the Jews to the market. They selected the professionals and placed them on a side. When the commandant asked me what was my trade, I told him that I was a watchmaker. Then he said, "Good, for the time being you will remain alive – go quickly to the right side!" Hundreds of Jews – women, children, and those "without a trade" remained standing on the left side. The police forced the unfortunate ones to lie in prepared pits, and then opened fire with a machine gun. After a while,

[Page 118]

the marketplace was full of dead bodies and rivers of blood. The peasants gathered around and quickly pillaged the dead as well as the wounded Jews. Everything took place before our eyes...

I will never forget this image...

Then, the commandant entered and said: "You Jews are guilty! The war broke out because of you. You will all be killed. However, for the time being, you are still useful – so you will remain alive in the interim"...

From there, we were sent to the Lida Ghetto. Rumors reached us that there were Jewish partisans in the surrounding forests, and anyone who could bring weapons with them would be accepted into the partisan group.

I decided to escape from the ghetto and go to the partisans. I succeeded in buying a gun for 30,000. I dismantled it into small pieces. One dark night, I and a group of 100 men cut the barbed wire fence and escaped from the Lida Ghetto. Our route passed through the large Naliboki Forest. According to our information, that is where the Jewish partisans were located. During the day[1], we hid in the thick parts of the forests, and we moved on further during the night. We encountered a patrol of the Jewish partisan group, which was under the command of the Bielski brothers from Nowogrudek. There were several hundred Jewish fighters in the camp, among them women and a few children. They [*i.e.*, the women and children] were involved in preparing food, fixing things, and other housekeeping tasks.

I was with Bielski's partisans for two years. Our work was to destroy bridges, railway lines, and other important military objects. [We also] would attack German or White Russian

[Page 119]

police stations or military points. We obtained food from nearby peasants according to a great protocol and system. This was all described well enough in the "Forest Jews" book that was published in Hebrew by the Bielski brothers (today living in the Land of Israel).

When the Russians drove the Germans out of eastern Poland, and we could emerge from [hiding in] the forests, I returned to Eishishok. In the town, I already found Shalom Sonenson, his brother Moshe and wife Tzipora, with their children, Tzirel Jurkanski's family, Sara Kabatznik and her family. I registered with the N.K.V.D. unit whose task was to clear the region of Polish white partisans and others who had collaborated with the Germans. I and Moshe Sonenson, who was with me in the same unit, took revenge on all the hooligans whose hands were dirty with Jewish blood. We recovered many Jewish stolen articles that we recognized. The gentiles who fell into our hands paid dearly.

During the first period, we captured small groups of German soldiers who were hiding in the surrounding forests during the time of the great German retreat. Once, we, a group of armed Jews, captured six Germans near Eishishok, among them an S.S. officer. We brought them to the old cemetery. We placed the S.S. officer at the side, and shot the other Nazis on the spot. The officer fell at our feet and began to cry and beg us to not kill him. He had a wife and children in Germany, and he never harmed Jews – so he claimed and kissed our boots. "You have a wife and children," shouted Moshe Sonenson, " and did we not also have wives and children, you scoundrel?! Did you

[Page 120]

bloody beasts have mercy on our parents, wives, and children? You want to live, murderer? You will not merit such!"... As he [Moshe] was speaking, he lifted up his gun and smashed his head with its butt. Then he dipped his hands in the blood, raised them heavenward, and said, "See, G-d, my hands have spilled the blood of the murderer! For my father, and for my mother, for my two brothers and sister! For my young child whom the Jews had to suffocate so as not to fall into the hands of the Nazi scoundrels! – Revenge for them all!"...

Thus did we take revenge upon many of those who ha collaborated with the Germans, and this cast a pall upon the gentiles. After some time, the Soviet military forces left Eishishok, and only three militias remained in the town. We happened to learn that white Polish partisans, who were hiding in the forests, were planning on mounting an attack against us, and that the gentiles in the town planned to join them when they arrived. We told a Russian captain who was passing through the town about the danger that was threatening us, and we asked him to send a division of soldiers to defend us. The captain tried to reassure us, saying that our "fear" was without merit. Such things do not take place under the Soviet regime, he told us, and with that he travelled onward.

We then decided to gather together in Shaul Sonenson's house, which was made of brick.

Indeed, a large group of Polish white partisans attacked us that night, together with a throng of gentiles of Eishishok. As long as we still had bullets, we were protected and kept the attackers at bay. However, when our bullets ran out, the murderers broke the doors and burst into the house.

[Page 121]

I jumped through a window in the attic, and set out for the orchard that was behind the house. The other Jews also escaped. I found Moshe Jurkanski, Mariashel's son, in the orchard. We ran through the gardens and the Pig Alleyway to the river, and hid the entire night among the bushes. In the morning, when it became light, we did not hear any shooting or shouting from the town, so we took the risk and returned to the town. We saw the destruction that the hooligans had perpetrated.

Moshe Sonenson's wife Feigele[2] and their young child had been murdered that night. They were hiding together with all the Jews in a dark side room. Because of the child, they could not escape. They heard the murderers breaking the furniture, looking for money. Then Feigele said to Moshe, "I recognize the voice of the Polish pharmacist. He knew father very well. He used to come to our home. I will go out to them, for in any case they will find us. Maybe they will have mercy on a woman with a young child?..."

That is what she did. However, as soon as she opened the door and the murderers saw her, they shot her and the child on the spot. They fell dead upon the doorstep. Hearing the shots and understanding what had taken place, Moshe Sonenson jumped out through a small window and fled to the surrounding forests. Thanks to that, he survived.

We, the few Jews, gathered together again after the pogrom. We sent word to the Jews of Radun, where there was still a Russian garrison. We told them what had taken place in Eishishok, and asked them to send a military division to us.

[Page 122]

When the military division arrived, we conducted searches among the gentiles of the town, and found our stolen goods with them. We arrested fifty gentiles and held them in what had been Yankel Kyoczewski's brick house (the former post office). A few days later, a large group of white partisans attacked again and freed the arrested gentiles. The exchange of shots between them and the Russians lasted an entire night. At dawn, the [white Polish] partisans fled into the forests. With time, things became calm. Life became normal. Polish shops opened in place of the Jewish ones. Also, Polish tradespeople, such as shoemakers, tailors, etc., came to Eishishok. A market once again took place on Thursdays, and gentiles did business with each other – they could manage without Jews. Poor gentiles from "Neien Plan," the Pigs Alleyway, or from nearby villages settled in the better houses. Our hearts were pained seeing how life went on normally, and we Jews were superfluous. However, seeing gentile men and women dressed in Jewish furs and clothing, and one could not do anything against them…

The hatred and the brazenness of the gentiles grew from day to day. They began to demand from the Soviet authorities that they punish us for our searches that we conducted, and accused us of stealing "their" goods. This was an infraction that was punished severely in Russia.

We felt that the earth had begun to burn under our feet. The Russian police commandant told me that it would be better for me, as well as for the remaining Jews, to leave Eishishok. I understood the hint, and decided to take his advice… I snuck across the Romanian border and came to the Land of Israel as a Ma'apil.[3]

Translator's Footnotes:

1.   The original says: "During the night." Checking the analogous translated Hebrew version (starting on page 82), and by logic, this was an error.

2.   The Yiddish name Feigele is equivalent with the Hebrew name Tzipora – and both names are used interchangeably in this testimony.

3.   A Ma'apil is a Jew who immigrated illegally to pre-state Israel in violation of British rule in the 1930s and 1940s - Aliyah Bet.

[Page 123]

Miscellaneous

[Page 124]

Blank

[Page 125]

The Rabbi and Gaon Rabbi Shimon Rozovski,
may G-d avenge his blood
The final rabbi of the community of Eishishok
(1874-1941)
(about his personality)

Translated by Jerrold Landau

Rabbi Shimon the son of Avraham was the son of pious parent from a family of Torah greats and rabbis. He was born in 1874 in the city of Kapyl (Kapoli), district of Minsk in White Russia.

Rabbi Shimon the son of Avraham was the son of pious parents from a family of Torah greats and rabbis. He was born in 1874 in the city of Kapyl (Kapoli), district of Minsk in White Russia.

He received a traditional Jewish education, as was customary in those days. When he got older, he studied in the famous Volozhin Yeshiva and later in the Yeshiva of Slobodka-Kovno.

He became known for his sharp mind and his great expertise in Gemara, Tosafot, and rabbinical responsa. He was brought in honor to his hometown of Kapyl to serve as the rabbi.

He was liked by the townsfolk, and he was accepted by all circles of the community. When the town was conquered by the Bolsheviks in 1919, he was forced to escape, for he was known as an enthusiastic Zionist. In 1921, the heads of the community of Eishishok asked him to fill the place of the Gaon Rabbi Yosef

Zundel Hutner of blessed memory, who had died two years previously, and left the town without a spiritual leader. He [Rabbi Rozovski] served in the rabbinate in Eishishok for twenty years, until the day of his tragic death along with thousands of members of his community, on 5 Tishrei, 5702 [1941]. May G-d avenge his blood.

Rabbi Shimon Rozovski did not cloister himself within the four ells of Torah. Rather, he was an important activist in the Mizrachi movement, and participated as a delegate in many conventions and gatherings of that party. He was also active in work on behalf of the national funds. He took an interest in the economic and communal life of the Eishishok community. He was among the doers and activists in every important communal endeavor. He spoke well and fulfilled [his obligations] well [*i.e.*, he not only spoke, but he acted].

He published many articles in Zionist newspapers both in Poland and in the Land of Israel. He prepared to publish a Torah book called *Shevet Shimon*, but the manuscript, like the author, was lost forever during the time of destruction.

[Page 126]

As has been said, Rabbi Shimon Rozovski was one of the few rabbis in Lithuania and Poland who bore the banner of Zionism up high and with pride. He did not flinch from the attacks of his rabbinical comrades, who, for the most part, tended toward the anti-Zionist Agudas Yisroel. He also knew how to befriend the youth and help them in their cultural and Zionist activities. He also wrote articles for *Unzer Fand* [Our Banner], that was published by the Jewish National Fund in Eishishok in 1936. He wrote the following among the rest of his words:

"… The Torah tells us 'and you shall take possession of it and settle in it.' [Numbers 33:53] It is our obligation to take possession of our land… We have no other path than to redeem our land with the best of our money, our fat, and our blood. Every person who donates to the Jewish National Fund [Keren Kayemet LeYisrael] redeems our Land every day, and fulfills the commandment 'and you shall take possession of it and settle in it.' Therefore, my heart is glad when I see that the honorable residents of my city are virtually all lovers of Zion, who fulfil this great commandment and support the Jewish National Fund. This is especially the case now, during these times, when the Jewish National Fund is making a great rectification, for all the residents on the lands owned by the Jewish National Fund are obligated to observe the Sabbath along with all the commandments dependent on the Land..."

When the booklet "The Charitable Fund" was published in Eishishok in 1936, we find in it an article written by him regarding the value of charitable deeds, for the heart of our rabbi was alert to all communal needs, large and small. He played an active role in everything, acting and urging others to act. He aroused the masses and urged them toward faithful communal activism.

However, the crowning achievement of his communal work was for the Refugee Committee, which he headed. Many eyewitnesses in this anthology have written about this. Thousands of refugees who passed through Eishishok at the beginning of the war owe him thanks for this assistance, and for perhaps also saving them from the danger of death at the hands of the Communist and Lithuanian police.

Thus did he stand at the head of the community of Eishishok for the last twenty years of his life and of the life of his community, until he drank from the poison cup, as he witnessed the destruction of his beloved community with his own eyes, and met his own death – the death of a martyr – among his unfortunate community members.

May his soul be bound in the bonds of eternal life.

[Page 127]

As a Fleeting Dream…

Yitzchak Ogen

Translated by Jerrold Landau

On a cold, snowy winter day, a young lad, approximately 18 years old, girded himself and emerged from the sled that stopped in the town courtyard next to the well. He stood for a moment to gird his bones, which were sore after a 25-kilometer journey from the railway station to his destination. The wagon driver did not wait until his sole passenger shook himself off properly. He hurried up and jumped off his platform, tossed the lad's heavy suitcase to the ground, grunted a sort of greeting, hurried back to his place, and set off on his way, pulling the rains and cracking the whip, forging a new path in the fresh, pure snow, as he disappeared from the eye on a small alleyway in a corner of the square yard. The lad remained standing in this white town, as his heart wondered and palpitated regarding what was to come. At that time, it seemed that the town was empty of its residents. The small, black houses stood in silence, peering with their caulked, closed, patched windows upon the streets, which were empty of people. Only the thin smoke spiraling up from the chimneys gave evidence to the presence of residents of the houses, dealing with their day-to-day lives. Suddenly, the lad noticed a scalding glance, and was taken aback as a person caught in his disgrace. As he turned his head, he noticed in the nearby window a face looking through the pane, with eyes staring at him, assessing him … wondering… He took hold of his suitcase, and, as gestured by the peering eyes, forged his way to that home to ask for the location of the house of the principal of the town's Hebrew school, Mr. Botwinik.

That young lad from Vilna served in that town, Eishishok, as a Hebrew teacher for a short period of only five weeks. For various reasons, he was forced to abandon his post and return to his home.

However, those five weeks are etched in his memory forever. When he remembers those days, and when the image of the town, its people, its youth, its children, and everything therein comes before his eyes... and it seems at times that this is merely a dream and nothing more. Indeed, this town did not appear before him as a dream...

* * *

[Page 128]

Twenty-five kilometers from the railway station, cut off from the central living arteries of the poor state, it seems at times that the distance is farther. Around a great desert, with much desolation, in this desolate heart a place of human habitation sprouts out before him, as an oasis in the desert. The landscape is unique, unlike other landscapes in the towns of Poland, for it is lacking forests. This made an impression upon him, emboldened him, and strengthened him.

Indeed, Eishishok, you seemed to me as an island in the heart of the desert, a town of Israel. A Jewish town sprouted up in the desert of the Polish Diaspora, wonderful in its kind, serving as a pure birthplace for a Hebrew lad dreaming of *aliya* to the Land (waiting for a certificate, like all Jewish lads in those days). It demonstrated the revival of the nation and the language. On its own, far from other Jewish settlements and even from Christian settlements, it had a Jewish life that had no shortage of images and splendor of the desired life that will eventually be there, there...

There was no community in the Diaspora of Poland where the vast majority of its residents, young and old, men and women alike, knew Hebrew as in Eishishok. That Hebrew School existed for nearly three generations, went through several forms and incarnations, and was transferred as an inheritance to its final owners. Three generations received a modern Hebrew education. Hebrew, almost like a spoken language, was on the mouths of all its residents. There is no doubt that the children already learned the language from their mothers, who put them to sleep with

Hebrew melodies and folksongs. All residents of Eishishok, as Zionists, as Mizrachi followers, as Bundists and Communists (for there were all types in the town, as was usual in Jewish communities of Poland), all of them were fans of Hebrew with their full heart. They supported it with their mouths as with their hearts. All of them knew Hebrew and loved to speak it. Even the stormy debates in the presence of the Hebrew teacher, the purpose of which was to change his mind or negate his influence, even they were in the purity of the Hebrew language. Such Hebrew personalities were found to me, the Hebrew teacher for a brief period, later only in the Land [of Israel], and even here, not in every place, and not with such enthusiasm, with such love, love for its own sake. I testify before the heavens and the earth that several innovations of the language, which I discovered in the Land, some of which I have not heard the likes of – were created in Eishishok for the needs of the time, for the needs of expression, the joy of speaking, and the necessity of speaking…

The   Hebrew   school   and   its   teachers   in   1925
In the center of the principal Botwinik, one of the active cultural doers of Eishishok

[Page 129]

Spread and woven before his soul was a complete Jewish town, the dream of a different reality and of a life that was not here. With a meager livelihood, poor in deeds, with lots of time on his hands, a complete Jewish community was spread out and the dream of leaving the place and planting himself in a different place was woven. Many lads uprooted themselves form Eishishok, with the vast majority settling in the Land of Israel. Letters that arrived from them became public property, passing from hand to hand, and serving as a source of joy and encouragement for complete months. At times when I went out at night, tired of conversation and heavy in ideas, to wander through the alleyways of the town, the reality turned into a legend for me. I did not know where I was, and what place this town had chosen for itself. I imagined orchards growing and sprouting from its alleyways. The sounds of the waves of the Mediterranean Sea rose to my ears. The mountains of Judea cast their large shadows on the belly of the town, on the well, the swipe and bucket of which penetrated as a flat into the night, the last color of the shepherds…

* * *

I left the town, and its image is etched in my heart. I bear its burden as a precious gift that cannot be assigned a value. As the image of the town comes before my eyes, two significant feelings tug at me. I see, in my consciousness, the town emptied of its residents. They all left and are all here in the Land, scattered in all the settlements and cities of the Land. On the other hand, my heart and I have a different desire: To visit the town once more, which dwells alone, as an oasis in the desert of the far-off Diaspora, and to find there, complete and standing in all its essence and charm – that same birth-hive that is etched in his languages, dreams, and ideas… until the end that was more bitter than all came. Until I have an opportunity to meet with a refugee, a native of Congress Poland, who told me and left no more space for a dream. There is no place for anything other than a singular feeling of horror, of boundless horror and love.

Eishishok was transferred to Lithuania at the beginning of the war. It served as a border city, as a large center for Jewish refugees who escaped from Poland and wanted to go to Vilna or Kovno, from where they would have a hope of setting out for the Land. Eishishok girded itself completely, as a unified effort, to assist the refugees. It received them, and provided them with everything they could, with its entire soul and resources. Nobody was opposed. No resident of the town ignored the tribulation.

[Page 130]

When isolated individuals, individuals only, asked for recompence for their toil (it is not that, Heaven forbid, they denied their help), the rabbi convened a large gathering in the synagogue, and imposed a great ban on the transgressors, with black candles and a curse…

Eishishok, this dear Jewish city, was completely destroyed, and is no more. It lived like a dream, and was erased like a dream.

Tel Aviv, July 20, 1948.

Yizkor
(In memory of my kindergarten children)

by Rachel Abiri (Strikovski)

Translated by Jerrold Landau

In the great deluge of blood that befell the world, my small town – my charming town with its five roads that all converged in the market square in the center of the city – also drowned. From the images of your good, pure Jews, in whose hearts burned the holy fire of love of their nation and its Torah, Jews who were not excited by grandeur, but rather lived their simple, upright lives with the toil of their hands and commerce. From among these precious personalities flutter the dear images of the Yoseles and the Sarales ["little Josephs and little Sarahs"], their childhood deliberations, their laughter and cries filling the room of "my kindergarten"… the first Hebrew kindergarten twenty years ago in my town of Eishishok.

Behold, I see you in front of my eyes as if alive… You Sarale Libati – your blue eyes always laughing, for they saw a world full of innocence and splendor. And your dimples on your round cheeks. Oh, I could kiss them! You were the center of the "group"! … And you, serious Mirele ["little Miriam"], with the black curls, looking upon the agony of the world. You .. were also successful in the games that you organized! … How, how, Sarale? – did cruel foul people snuff out the wick of your young life! And you, Gitele Kumin – the famous "artiste"!

I remember the first Purim play of my kindergarten that we performed in the house of Jurditzinski (The Freiseliche). For the first time in your short life, you marched on the boards of the stage that was set up with love and dedication by Motke Burstin and Yankele, the son of the smith, according

[Page 131]

to all the "technical wisdom" in their hands. You ascended the stage, you, four years old, with strength, without fear. You recited, sang, and acted like a veritable "artiste." Your parents and your entire audience who heard and saw you rejoice in joy and were full of satisfaction [*naches*]. All foresaw a great future for you – an exemplary actress!

The crowding was so great that Leibele, the son of Leizer Remz, could not ascend the stage to "play his role"… and his father placed him on his shoulders and from that "stage" he flawlessly recited his declamation, without fear of the audience, and earned a stormy applause.

Then came the turn of the "Gypsy girl dance."

Mirale the daughter of Esther Kiuczewski, dressed in your colorful costume, "literally" a gypsy girl, started to dance. Your small feet took mincing steps on the boards of the stage… and you brought the audience of mothers and fathers to exceptional amazement and emotion!

And behold, you too, "our hero" – the oldest son of Batya and Tzvi Kopelman – I have forgotten your name – as twenty years have already passed since then!![1]

All of the children of the kindergarten were afraid of your small fists. More than once, I had to scold you for your acts of mischief. How is it now! Did you grow up and become a mighty man? Did you merit to repay the impure ones their just deserts, and take revenge for your parents, your family members, and all the residents of your town, as one of the partisans?

And perhaps you remained alive as one of the Holocaust survivors, and succeeded in coming to the Land [of Israel], and are among the camp of builders of the new homeland??...

Where are you all? I do not remember all your names now. The vicissitudes of life have caused me to forget them. However, your memories are alive in my heart, and I will remember you will love and reverence all the days of my life…

Aliya from Eishishok to the Land of Israel
(memories)

by Uri Rozovski

Translated by Jerrold Landau

This was in 1925. The situation of the Jews of Poland became more serious, and their economic situation was literally catastrophic. This was the well-known "Grabski era"[2]. The Zionist movements with all its streams and factions ruled the

Jewish street, and the aspiration of the masses of Jews, especially the youth, was *aliya* [emigrating] to the Land of Israel.

[Page 132]

One bright day, news spread in the town that the family of Zeev Sznider, one of the honorable families with many children, was preparing to make *aliya* to the Land.

This news had a novelty to it. A well-off Jew, honorable in his community, was abandoning his hometown, liquidating his assets, and preparing to settle in the Land of Israel... The Zionist parties regarded this event as a singular opportunity to demonstrate the love of their townsfolk for the Land of Israel.

A committee was set up to organize a large farewell celebration. The night of the farewell celebration arrived. It was a black, dark night, but suddenly the windows of the houses lit up with candelabras and candles. Members of the Zionist youth organizations -- Hechalutz, Hechalutz HaMizrachi, Hechalutz Hatzair, and Hashomer Hatzair – appeared in formation in lines, with torches in their hands. Each organization was in its designated spot. All of the organizations carried their flag and mottoes... Then the Sznider family left their house, surrounded by crowds from the city, relatives, acquaintances, and ordinary Jews. A large parade took place, with riders in front, and formations of youths with their flags behind them, singing songs of Zion. The streets were lit up like day, and the joy and emotions were very great.

The procession stopped at the edge of Radun Street, on the road leading to the Bastuny railway station[3], next to the house of Meir the Teacher. The rabbi of the city, Rabbi Shimon Rozovski, one of the veteran activists of Mizrachi in the district of Vilna, delivered a farewell speech, with his face beaming from joy and emotion. He spoke warm, enthusiastic words about the love of Zion and the revival of the nation. When he finished, he kissed the head of the family, Mr. Zeev Sznider. Then, leaders of the Zionist organizations spoke. Zeev Sznider and his son Shaul, the founder of the Hashomer Hatzair chapter in the city, responded to the blessings and greetings. The townsfolk then bid farewell to those making *aliya*, with the singing of *Hatikva*[4] by the thousands in attendance, with tears streaming from the eyes of many. All of those gathered returned to the town. All the organizations arranged themselves, gathered together, and returned to their meeting places. The sounds of song and dance of the local Zionist youth could be heard until a late hour. That evening was indeed an evening of great impression and essence. It was spoken of for a long time.

However, there were other results of that evening. The Polish priest and the town physician,

[Page 133]

great anti-Semites, complained to the head of the district government in Lida about the police chief of Eishishok for granting permission for the Jews to organize a "Zionist demonstration" and disturb the sleep of the calm residents until a late hour of the night...

Incidentally, the police chief was an apostate Jew who had a very positive attitude to the Zionist movement. He was fired for this, and a new police chief was appointed, whose relations were more exacting and stringent. Nevertheless, the impression of the "Zionist demonstration" did not depart from the hearts of the townsfolk for a long time, and brought many people close to the Zionist idea.

[Page 134]

My Shtetl

by Mordechai Kaleko

Translated by Jerrold Landau

My native shtetl, you innocent victim,
The hands of the enemy did not pass over you
People like beasts – barbaric, corrupt
Turned you into a bloody field.

The market with shops, the houses were set on fire –
My shtetl, I will never see you again…
Deep in my heart sit the wounds,
A tear and another tear fall from the eyes…

The wind from the wide forests blows
Colorful wreaths of flowers, twist;
Among the fields, sown with grain
I would sing and dance joyfully there.

Everyone relaxed there near the small stream,
Not thinking about, not knowing of the danger,
The green meadows, the trees on the hill
Were G-d's finest gift…

My shtetl was beautiful on the Sabbath early morning
When Jews walked calmly from the synagogue,
visiting…
Children played around Jewish houses – – –
Where are you now??? – murdered, murdered…

I see my town on Sabbath eves –
From the Sabbath rest, from the walls,
The youth walk the streets in song – – –
Where are you now??? – tortured, burnt…

Oy! The day turned into a dark night…
I see the destruction from afar – – –
Will the bestial regime pay for it?!
With the revenge for those times come soon???

Translator's Footnotes:

1.   Editor: In the Lithuanian State Historical Archives, at LVIA/1817/1/23, there is a reference to a "Berko" [Ber], the son of Hirsz and Basia Kopelman, who was born on April 4, 1928. In Eastern Europe, the Yiddish given name of Hirsz / Hirsh was often paired with the Hebrew given name of Tzvi, as both have the same meaning.

2.   Władysław Dominik Grabski (1874 – 1938) served as the prime minister of Poland in 1920 and from 1923 to 1925. https://en.wikipedia.org/wiki/W%C5%82adys%C5%82aw_ Grabski

3.   Editor: The Bastuny station was on the Vilna-Lida railway line.

4.   Editor: "The Hope," today Israel's national anthem.

NAME INDEX

Y

Z